JAPANESE FINE ARTS

TOURIST LIBRARY: 9

TOURIST LIBRARY

Volumes Already Published

Volumes in Preparation

"Matsu-Taka Zu" (Pine-tree and Hawk) (part) by *Eitoku Kanō*

(Academy of Fine Arts in Tōkyō)

JAPANESE FINE ARTS

BY

Prof. TOKUZŌ SAGARA

JAPAN TRAVEL BUREAU

TŌKYŌ

JAPANESE FINE ARTS
  Copyright, 1955, by
Japan Travel Bureau.
  Printed in Japan by
Kyōdō Printing Co., Tōkyō.

First edition :   June, 1949
Second edition :   November, 1953
Third edition :   March, 1955

EDITORIAL NOTE

The purpose of the Tourist Library Series is to give foreigners interested in Japan a basic knowledge of various phases of Japanese culture. When completed, the Series is expected to include a hundred volumes or so, and will give a complete picture of Japanese culture, old and new.

Each volume in the Library is the work of a recognized authority on the subject, and it is hoped that by perusing these studies of Japanese life the reader will gain some insight into the unique culture that has developed in this country throughout the ages.

The present volume, " Japanese Fine Arts," is the work of Prof. Tokuzō Sagara, dean of the College of Culture in Miyazaki University. He is an outstanding authority on both Western and Japanese fine arts, and is the author of several books on the history of painting.

The text of the present volume was originally written in Japanese. Our special thanks are due to Mr. Senkichiro Katsumata, emeritus professor of Waseda University, who translated the manuscript into English, and to Miss K. Nakabayashi who looked over the translation. We also take great pleasure in expressing our indebtednes to all the institutions and individuals that kindly allowed us to use their photographs.

THE EDITOR

June, 1953

CONTENTS

CONTENTS

PLATE I

"Flowers and
Birds of the Seasons"
(Pair of screens)
Attrib. to *Shugetsu*

FOREWORD

Tourists from the United States and Europe traveling in Japan may have had occasion to see Japanese objects of art in the art galleries and museums in Tōkyō, Kyōto, and Nara, in the Shintō shrines and Buddhist temples in various parts of the country, and in the residences of many collectors of art treasures. I presume that these foreigners will invariably have a feeling of unfamiliarity regarding these art specimens, at least for some time after they first observe them. This is because, Japanese art is in various respects, so different from European art or anything falling under that category.

Speaking of painting, which occupies the leading and central position among the various branches of art, the themes treated are different from those of the West. In Japanese art, for instance, instead of Christ, Virgin Mary, and the martyrs, Buddha, Kannon (*Avalokitesvara* in Skr.), Bosatsu (*Bodhisattva*, and their high priests are portrayed, and recluses such as Rōshi (Lao-tsze) and Sōshi (Chwang-tsze), Chinese mystics, are depicted with a spirit of reverence. Needless to say, this choice of subject matter, as well as the spirit in which it is done by the Japanese painter is connected with the history of the religious and spiritual life of the nation. Strictly speaking, a foreigner must have some knowledge of this history before he can appreciate Japanese art. In the color prints, where scenes from the everyday life of the common people are treated, it is superfluous to point out that, the customs and manners therein represented being entirely unlike those seen in Europe, the art depicted must of necessity be different from the genre paintings of the Dutch or those in the rococo style.

The difference of themes is one of the prime factors in giving Japanese paintings a something that strikes the uninitiated with a peculiar feeling of strangeness. This, however, should not hinder the esthetic appreciation of Japanese art.

When the foreigner becomes a little accustomed to the medium in which the themes are rendered, he will soon be able to regard the pictures with a proper appreciation, even if he is little acquainted with the history of Japanese thought and customs. The important thing in Japanese painting is the difference of ideals. Unlike the laws governing Western painting, Japanese painting puts no emphasis on scientific and rational realism. This has been the tradition since the art of painting was introduced into the country from China ten centuries ago. In painting characters, natural scenery, houses or flowers, the object aimed at is grasping the essentials or their conventionalized forms, and not exactness or realism in portrayal. In this grasping of the essentials there is seen a direct adherence to Chinese ideals in painting, these being chiefly represented by black-ink paintings — for instance, in the natural scenery, flower-and-bird paintings of the Muromachi period (1392—1568) or the so-called *Nanga* paintings of the Edo period (1615—1867). Conventionalization in painting is the ideal adopted by the Japanese painters in the period when the influence of China was waning. That tendency is conspicuous, for instance, in the *Yamato* school of painting dating from the Heian period (794—-1185) or the conventionalized paintings of the Edo period.

It is but natural that these two ideals in painting should have brought into being a means of expression different from that of the realistic painting of Europe. In Japanese painting stills lack a background entirely and in scenery perspective is entirely ignored, and in the painting of solids, no shading is used. Instead, the brush-lines peculiar to Japanese painting are held to be of chief importance. This different technique in artistic expression may contribute to the strange feelings in the mind of the foreign observer of Japanese paintings. The last and most important point to be mentioned is the difference between the materials and brushes used by Japanese painters and those used by their Western brothers in the art. The former include paper, silk, Indian ink, and colors diluted in water instead of in oil; and the *fude*, a brush made quite differently from those used by the artists of the West. One clear-cut result of the use of these materials and the *fude* is a simplicity and cleanliness not to be observed in European frescos and oil paintings. Even in gorgeous flower-and-bird paintings, there is a more definite atmosphere of simplicity and cleanliness than there is in similar European paintings. This characteristic has a natural and fairly important connection with the genesis of the expressive technique peculiar to Japanese paintings, as has already been mentioned. In expressing the roundness of a thing, for instance, instead of making use of shading, the Japanese painter accomplishes his purpose solely by the use of brush-lines. In the painting of characters, scenes from nature, houses, animals, or plants, the outlines are invariably represented by brush-lines, and in the pigmentation the lines are never painted over, so they stand out as beautiful features appealing to the eye. This is possible only when the brush is adapted for free movement in all directions, when high-quality Indian ink is mixed with water on the ink-stone, and smooth paper or silk is used.

The size of Japanese paintings which is regulated by the use to which they are put may be another factor contributing to their strangeness to Western eyes. The proportion between length and breadth is not in accordance with the " gold cut " of European paintings; the works of Japanese artists appear either as vertically long paintings, such as *kakemono* (hanging pictures) or horizontally long ones such as picture scrolls. In spite of these differences that strike Westerners at first with a feeling of strangeness, Japanese paintings are decidedly worthy of serious consideration. Specimens of Japanese art have been on show in international exhibitions held in London since the middle of the 19th century and their exotic charms have pleased the artistic sense of Western lovers of beauty. Moreover, there are indications that Japanese paintings have given fruitful suggestion to painters of the impressionist and the post-impressionist schools and other specialists in art. This is substantiated by the fact that distinguished critics of art in Europe and America have often made the same statement.

The object I have in view at present is to set forth some ideals that may prove useful as a guide to those yet uninitiated in Japanese art, especially painting. It is not my plan to make a historical survey of art in Japan, tracing its development in a systematic way. There are already some such treatises on the market, and no addition is called for. My objective is to present a number of fundamental ideas necessary for the understanding and appreciation of Japanese paintings and other arts and to state them in as practical and effective a manner as possible.

With these brief remarks by way of a foreword, I now proceed with the treatment of the subject before me.

I. BLACK-INK PAINTINGS AND
BRUSH-LINES

To the Western eye " Sumi-e ", monochrome pictures in black, are perhaps one of the most curious of Japanese paintings. In *sumie* there is a certain amount of shading variety in the black. In the West pictures in black and white are popular as our readers all know. Etchings and dessins fall under this category.

However, etchings and dessins are not impressive enough to be placed in the same rank as frescos and oil paintings. The canvas is usually small. But in Japanese monochrome paintings, the scale is often pretentious; the pictures are often painted on large *kakemono* for display in the alcove and also on *fusuma*, or sliding screens, usually in a set of four, or on folding screens (*byōbu*) consisting of two sections or a pair of six sections. Thus Japanese monochrome pictures can be of impressive worth, lending themselves naturally to such large-scale canvases. Visitors to Japan from abroad will have abundant opportunity to see excellent specimens of these black-ink paintings in the historic temples and in the ancient mansions of former feudal lords.

This art came originally from China. There are two schools of monochrome painting. One is the *Hokuga* (paintings of the north) school, which dates from the Muromachi period (1392—1568). This school followed the precepts of the painters of the academy of north China in the Sung and Yūan periods (10th—14th cent.). The other is the *Nanga* (paintings of the south) school, which was brought into being in the middle of the Edo period (1615—1867). Pictures by artists of this school are also known as literary pictures, as the artists were usually men of letters. This school was founded by amateurs, men of letters who flourished in south China in the Ming and Ch'ing periods (14th—19th cent.). In Japan the *Hokuga* school is represented by artists flourishing in the Muromachi period—Shūbun, Sesshū, Shūgetsu, Sesson, and Nōami, and by their successors, the illustrious painters of the Kanō family —Masanobu, Motonobu, and Eitoku in the Momoyama period (1568—1615) and Tan-yū and Naonobu in the Edo period.

Now what is the difference between the monochrome paintings of the *Hokuga* school and the amateur paintings of the *Nanga* school? Inferring from the fact that the *Hokuga* school of painting had its development among the professional painters of the Chinese academy of painting, one might be apt to consider the art as demonstrating petty technique full of needless niceties in artificiality, but in reality such was not always the case. In the Japanese

FIG. 1 "Dharma and His Disciple"   by Sesshū
(Sainenji Temple, Aichi pref.)

FIG. 2 "Dharma" by Keishoki (Shōkei)

(Nanzenji Temple, Kyōto)

monochrome paintings at least, a decided opposite is the case. This is plainly attested to by the fact that the leading monochrome painters in the Muromachi period, such as Shūbun, Sesshū, Shūgetsu, Sesson, and Keishoki, were priests of the Zen sect of Buddhism who had little to do with artificiality, or, as in the case of Nōami, Masanobu, or Motonobu, men who set great store by the teachings of Zen. Zen is the most important of the Buddhist sects; it teaches the emancipation of the soul from a miscellany of worldly thoughts and its union with the truth of the world and life.

This doctrine is reflected in the choice of motif made by these monochrome painters. Their most characteristic theme is Daruma (*Dharma*), an Indian priest of distinction, who, tradition says, went to China to spread the Zen doctrine which he had been taught by Buddha himself. Needless to say, pictures of Daruma were not painted realistically, with revered Indian saint posing as a model. What the painters were taught was to express through their fancy of the features of Daruma the subtleties of Zen they had succeeded in grasping. Accordingly, when we look at the pictures of Daruma as depicted by these artists, we are supposed to see how each one comprehended the doctrine and greatness of Daruma; in other words, just how great was the depth of their emancipation and penetration. The value of the paintings is judged on this basis. Take, for instance, the Daruma painted by Sesshū (1420—1507). (See

Fig. 1.) In it one perceives the manifestation of a mighty power which only a saint who has attained the realm of absolute mental freedom can possess, a power that is super-human in character. The piercing eyes and the firmly closed lips which are symbolic of a strong will suggest such an idea. It may safely be presumed that Sesshū, who crossed the sea to study Zen in China and who occupied the foremost position in the T'iengt'ung Temple, had at least a glimpse of the lofty realm which the soul of Daruma had attained. Keishoki (15th—16th cent.) also used Daruma as the subject of many of his paintings. (Fig. 2.) He resembles Sesshū in his depiction of the sharp eyes and the firm lips that indicate a stout will. But from a Japanese point of view, the Daruma pictures by Keishoki lack a fullness of spirit; and when one compares them with the features of quiet simplicity and aloofness expressed in the Daruma paintings by Sesshū. one is tempted to conclude that the enlightenment Keishoki had acquired was not so elevated as that of Sesshū.

Next to Daruma the most popular subjects selected by the monochrome painters were portraits of Japanese priests of high spiritual attainment, especially those connected with such historic Zen temples as the Daitokuji and Tōfukuji in Kyōto. It is to be supposed that, being contemporaries of the painters, these priests were treated realistically by them in their portraits, which, therefore, may be considered as real likenesses of the priests in feature and figure.

FIG. 3 Portrait of Daitō Kokushi
(Daitokuji Temple, Kyōto)

FIG. 4 Portrait of Shōichi Kokushi
(Tōfukuji Temple, Kyōto)

However, likeness alone is not the object aimed at in such portraits; there must also be depicted the individual characteristics and the depth of spiritual enlightenment attained by the subject. It is in this sense that the portraits of Daitō Kokushi (Founder of the Daitokuji Temple; died, 1337) and Shōichi Kokushi (Founder of the Tōfukuji Temple; 1202—1280) are held to be masterpieces by art critics. (Fig. 3, 4.)

"Kanzan Jittoku" is another favorite theme for the monochrome artist. (Pl. 2) Kanzan and Jittoku were recluse-poets of China, who enjoyed a life of high thinking in Zen philosophy and primitive plain living in their home in a secluded ravine in the heart of the mountains. In the delineation of these characters, the artist tried to produce an atmosphere in which simplicity is the keynote, so that the life and soul of the recluses might stand out.

The same things may be said of "Chikurin Shichiken" (Seven Sages in a Bamboo Grove). (Pl. 3) These seven sages of China are said by tradition to have lived a clean life, free from greed and passion, and unhampered by the cares of the wicked world. Their favorite resort was a spot in a bamboo grove, where they gave themselves up to playing music, composing poems, and painting pictures. The theme, therefore, could be treated successfully only by those painters who could appreciate such a way of living and such a mentality.

Natural scenery was a theme much more popular

with the monochrome painters than the characters mentioned above. Pictures with such a theme are called *sansui* (lit. water and mountains), and in each a towering mountain, a ragged rock, trees not over-clustered, and a humble, grass-thatched dwelling form a composition. These landscapes, as one may expect, are radically different from those by Western artists, which are usually realistic, whether the subject be a mountain, a wood, a street corner, or a house.

FIG. 5 "Angling by a River" by Motonobu Kanō
(Reiur.-in Monastery, Kyōto)

Landscapes by Chinese or Japanese artists, on the other hand, represent the fancy and the imaginative genius of their limners. That is to say, the pictures rendered are expressive of the ideals and the longings of their authors; in other words, the monochrome painting is nothing but the visual expression of the Utopia of its exponent. The Utopias of the artists are not places of worldly pleasures, nor regions exuding a modern atmosphere, but quiet spots "far from the mudding crowd" basking in the lap of nature and loved so dearly by Kanzan and Jittoku, the Chinese recluses referred to above. For an example one may point out "San-ekisai Zu" (Before the House of a Recluse) by Shūbun (14th—15th cent.), in which a couple of pine-trees are shown at the foot of a steep rocky hill, where nestles a house in the Chinese style. (Pl. 4) In the small space in front of the house stands a servant, simple-minded and free from greed, sweeping the ground with a broom. "Kakei Sansui" (Summer Landscape) by Sesshū, to cite another instance, shows a group of rugged rocks with a broad expanse of blue sky. (Pl. 5) The same love of nature is seen in "Sansui Zu" (Landscape) by Shūgetsu (d. c, 1510) and the "Kōhan Suichō Zu" (Angling by a River) by Motonobu (1496—1559). (Fig. 5) In a word, the monochrome artists used their pictures as a medium to express the fancies that well up in their minds showing that they find enjoyment in things transcendental, reclusive, and serene.

這裡

平生

三讀

兩

个

However, something worldly and human is indispensable also in these imaginary landscapes (*sansuiga*). Whenever found advisable, a house or persons are added. In this respect pictures of flowers and birds are perhaps more transcendental. Birds hovering among trees or flowers possess no minds. They are said to have a feature in common with the mentality of the saint who is free from worldly concerns —at least in appearance. Such an interpretation may be offered as the reason why the monochrome painters took such a fancy for depicting flowers and birds. Besides, trees and flowers are attractive, being themselves things of beauty.

The esthetic qualities of these objects come not only from their features, that is, their form, but also from their coloring. This accounts for the practice of using pigmentation sometimes even in monochrome pictures. The coloring used in such cases is, of course, not deep, but extremely light. Gorgeous coloring in flower-and-bird paintings was the rule in other schools of art; for instance, a school of decorative artists which had its beginning in the Momoyama period (1568—1615). The artists in the Muromachi period (1392—1568) were fully content with the occasional addition of color to their productions which are characterized solely by the variation of light and shade in one color, black.

In this connection, let us examine pictures of flowers and birds on the folding screen by Shūgetsu. (Pl. 1) There is in one of his pictures a waterside scene with stones set here and there. Trees bare of leafage bend their branches toward the surface of water, and, as supplementary features, reeds, *omoto (Rhodea japonica)* and other plants are pictured. In among these plants a pheasant, light and quick-witted, walks with its head raised. Mandarin ducks, in pairs as usual, are swimming peacefully in the water. There are swallows flying through the air with the speed of wind and a small bird with a pretty-colored tail perched on a branch. All are without volition, in complete harmony with nature. What we observe in such a picture is the expression of the mood of the artist.

Considered in this way, the monochrome painting of the *Hokuga* school in the Muromachi, Momoyama, and Edo periods should not be described as an art full of artificiality, whose artists took pride in the technical ingenuity of their execution which is the criticism of some art authorities. In this respect there seems to be no substantial difference between these paintings and the amateur art of the *Nanga* school which found favor among the literati. Of the *Nanga* school a fuller exposition will be made later on. Here let a word suffice. The *Nanga* school also aims at the representation of the state of mind using serenity as its keynote. Between the two, however, there is this difference: while in the monochromes of the *Hokuga* school importance is placed on severe and powerful brush-lines, in pictures of the *Nanga* school, soft brush-lines, suitable for the expression of the spirit of transcendence, so much valued by the literary painters, are in great favor.

As brush-lines are the basic structure of all branches of painting in Japan, it may be pertinent here to give an introductory explanation of them. Some of our readers, perhaps, have seen a Japanese painting brush, and may have noticed that it is constructed differently from the brush of the painter in oils. It is a conical tuft of the hair of a small animal, such as the hare or the badger, fixed firmly at the end of a bamboo tube. The hair absorbs the ink in readiness for painting. The ink is a fluid prepared by rubbing *sumi* (a stick made of the black of burn-

Modern *Sumie* Painter in His Atelier

ing pine-wood mixed with high-quality resin) on an ink-stone containing some water. The point of the brush, dabbed in ink, because of the flexible animal hair and its pointed conical shape, lends itself readily to movement in any direction desired, with any degree of pressure, speed, or angle. When the brush is applied with a slight pressure, so that only the point touches the paper lightly, a slender line is produced. When the pressure is heavy, the line produced is thick. No elaborate explanation is needed about the result of the speed of the brush. A high speed makes the line generally quick and lively, sometimes frivolous or wild. On the contrary, a low speed produces lines that are suggestive of heaviness, solidity, composure, or fortitude.

There is difficulty in giving a satisfactory explanation to the uninitiated foreigner of the angle at which the brush is held when painting. An attempt will be made here. When the brush is moved in the position of right angles with the piece of paper or silk, the line drawn is simple, and hard like a piece of wire. When moved in a slanting position, the line drawn is generally considered to be weak. But this is a crude way of putting it. The line in this case, to a knowing observer, is much more complicated in analysis. To be precise, the line produced by the brush point is vigorous, while that part of the line drawn by the side, technically called *hara* or belly, is weak and hollow in suggestion. In one and the same line there are combined these two divergent elements, which, instead of showing a contrast, are shaded by gradation from strength to weakness. The general impression produced, therefore, is that the line drawn by the brush held slantingly is weaker than drawn with the brush held upright. This line, complicated in character, has its own rôle to play in painting.

If the painter dips the brush in water when he starts painting, touches the ink with the end of the brush, and then proceeds to draw a line, that line, whether long or short, will be one in which the black color fades out with almost imperceptible gradation. It is necessary to add that in this case the slanted brush is held at right angles to the direction in which it is moving. This case is elaborated on here as it is the basic stroke. The shading of the line naturally changes when the angle is changed in accordance with the direction in which the brush is moving. By making frequent use of such a method the artist can represent the roundness of a thing by a single stroke. A round jewel, *hōshu*, is often realistically pictured, without resorting to shading, by such a circular line. Picturing the *hōshu* jewel was the first lesson in painting assigned to a pupil by his master in many private art schools as it constitutes the basic exercise in the use of the brush. Such antiquated methods are of course no longer in use in art schools where instruction is based on a modern methodical plan, but it is said that the *hōshu* jewel exercises were employed until the end of the Meiji era

(1868—1912) and were the chief assignment for beginners for two or three years in many private art schools, to the utter weariness and discouragement of the pupils.

As has been explained above, all lines may be classified on the basis of direction, pressure, speed, and the brush angle. This is theoretically correct. Lines drawn on paper or silk may be considered as various combinations of those "dynamic" elements, so that the feelings that come from lines are of infinite variety. To these variations another factor

FIG. 6 "Scroll of Landscape" (part)

should be added—the method of holding the brush. The usual method is to hold a brush with the thumb and two or three fingers, not using the little finger. When held tightly, the brush moves stiffly, and, when held too loosely, it slips from the control of the painter, and moves unsteadily and sluggishly. There is yet another factor in causing variations and that is the position of the wrist. To this is to be added another—the angle and the height of the arm. With so many factors contributing to the making of variation in lines, the foreigner may understand how

by Sesshu (Collection of Mr. M. Mori, Tōkyō)

infinite are the feelings that are expressible by mere strokes of the paint-brush. Varied as may be the feelings expressed by varying lines, those used by individual artists have their own characteristics. Such is the conclusion derived from observation. This is, I believe, a point that will be readily agreed upon by foreigners who have had some initiation in the Japanese art of painting. This individual characteristic in lines is a reliable test as to whether the signature on a picture is authentic or otherwise. This individuality of lines is based on the bony structure, sinews, and nerves of the maker of those lines and these cause the physiological and psychological conditions of the painter. To put it in another way, which perhaps shows a firmer grasp of the truth, the line is the man himself. Painters of gentle disposition are apt to draw gentle lines, while those of sterner disposition are inclined to draw strong lines. Here of course the cultural attainments of the artists play a part, for culture to a slight degree and in slow gradation has the power of modifying the individuality of the artist. The Japanese are accustomed to the brush not only in painting but also in writing, and we are firm in the belief that there is a close connection between the man and his brush strokes.

We now return to the monochrome painters of the Muromachi and Momoyama periods. One feature common to both periods is the sternness and strength of their lines. There is a range of individual variation, which naturally forms the basis of judgment

PLATE VI   "Screen Picture of Lions"

Eitoku Kanō

regarding the genuineness of the productions of the old masters. Such subtleties are unnecessary for a general appreciation of Japanese paintings for the average foreigner. Only the general characteristics of the monochrome paintings need to be considered here. As instances of the typical pictures illustrating the severity, sternness, and strength of lines, one may cite only two out of many. One is Sesshū's "Sansui Zukan" (Scroll of Landscape) (Fig.6). In a section of this masterpiece, that is, on the extreme left where his signature is seen, there is in the foreground a large cliff and in the far distance, a rocky, steep hill standing against a dark sky, with a path running now visible, now out of sight, between rocks on either side. The other is "Karajishi Zu Byōbu" (Screen Picture of Lions) by Eitoku Kanō (1543—1590). (Pl. 6) Especially noticeable are the lines used in depicting the lions. Unlike the hardness which is characteristic of a rock, the skin of a lion is organic in nature, and the lion itself is no more than an animal, though his fierce appearance entitles him to be styled king of the beasts. In spite of this the lines used in the painting of the beasts are appalling in their strength; they may be compared to steel wires.

The severity, sternness, and strength of the lines in these monochromes are not easily achieved by anyone. Technically speaking, considerable skill is necessary before one can attain perfection in these. The objective is only attained when one has the mastery of a Sesshū or an Eitoku. Here the point may be admitted as true that, compared with the pictures of the *Nanga* school which began its existence as amateur art of the literati, the monochrome pictures of the *Hokuga* school are characterized by professionalism. Be that as it may, the authors of the most vigorous lines in the monochrome paintings were Zen priests or those who were strongly influenced by Zen teachings, and this fact suggests the conclusion that their rigorous Zen training had something to do with the production of these masterful lines.

The monochromes with their characteristic lines symbolic of severity, sternness, and strength, attained a high development under the patronage of the Muromachi Shoguns, who, it appears, had leanings toward Zen doctrines. The popularity of these monochrome pictures continued into the Edo period (1615—1867), though the circumstances under which they were maintained, were somewhat different from those in the preceding period. They flourished because the Shogun reigning in Edo, who had the idea that the severe features of the monochrome pictures suited the tastes and esthetic characteristics of the *samurai* class, appointed Tan-yū Kanō (1602—1674) as painter-in-ordinary of his court. That position was held by successors of Tan-yū up until the Restoration of the Imperial rule at the beginning of the Meiji era. Though the family failed to produce any painter of genius except its illustrious founder, it continued its efforts to spread the art of monochrome painting.

FIG. 8

FIG. 7

" Hawks on Pine-branches " by
Sesson (op. 1544—1589)
(National Museum of Tokyo)

Feudal lords of great influence, such as the clans of Kanazawa, Kagoshima, and Sendai, and also minor lords throughout the country held in great esteem the monochrome pictures of the Kanō family and took back to their clans pupils of the Kanō artists giving them residence and patronage in return for their services in art and painting. The art become popular with all ranks of the *samurai* class and, even among the ordinary townsmen, it had its devotees. This accounts for the generous numbers of monochromes in the country, which are found so universally that a foreign tourist in even a remote country town can feast his eyes on one or more excellent monochrome specimens almost any house which has a claim to historic origin.

"Kakitsubata Zu Byōbu" (Irises)

II. CONVENTIONALIZED FLOWERS AND BIRDS

The reader may have noticed young Japanese women walking along a street in Tōkyō or in other town dressed in the prettily patterned native costume. He may have observed that the *kimono*, *obi*, *haori* (coat) and *han-eri* (collar of an underwear of *kimono*) which make up their attire are adorned with large conventionalized flowers, charming little birds, trees, or waves. On occasions such as a formal visit to a friend or going to a play or a concert, young ladies wear *kimonos* in which the patterns are much more gorgeous in design and brighter in color. Such patterns are not reserved for young ladies alone; even in the case of elderly women, if one looks closely enough, one will find them all there in their dresses — only the patterns are smaller and more subdued in color. The reader must not overlook the fact, when he is invited to a Japanese home, that on objects in everyday use, such as a small lacquered case, an inkstone box, a small dinner table, wooden bowls, china vessels for confections, and china bowls, the same conventionalized patterns are in evidence.

FIG. 9 Folding Screen showing Water-fowl on a Beach

These patterns so intimately associated with the daily life of the Japanese have been taken from the various decorative paintings originating in the Momoyama period (1368—1615). From that time to the beginning of the Edo period (1615—1867) there was an age when, all wars having ceased, industry was revived and a brisk trade with China, Luzon, and Java was carried on. Our forefathers in those days had their first taste of the wealth and culture of the West through those countries. One can easily

by Sansetsu (Collection of Mr. I. Hosotsuji, Kyōto)

imagine the vivacity and brilliance of the life of the people of those days.

It was in such a period that our decorative painting had its birth. The first master of this branch of art was Eitoku Kanō (1543—1590). Being an artist of the *Hokuga* school of painting, he worked with the usual monochrome pictures with their stern and severe style, but he also produced those gorgeous decorative pictures, such as "Matsu-Taka Zu" (Pine-tree and Hawk) and "Ryū-o Shunsō Zu" (Willow,

Cherry-tree, and Spring Flowers), which are done in bright colors on magnificent folding screens. (See the frontispiece and the illustration between p. 42 and 43.) Next to him in merit comes Sanraku Kanō (1559—1635), Eitoku's adopted son. Among Sanraku's numerous masterpieces are "Setchū Ryūro Zu" (Willow and Herons in a Snowy Scene) and "Suihen Ro Zu" (Herons beside a Pond). Sanraku also had an adopted son Sansetsu Kanō (1590—1651). His

FIG. 10 Sansetsu's Water-fowl

is a name that cannot be omitted from a history of Japanese painting since he is a great artist possessing a style of his own. In his "Kaihin Suikin Zu Byōbu" (Folding Screen showing Water-fowl on a Beach), one sees a decorative painting almost ideal in conception and execution, the composition embracing fantastically crooked pine boughs, a flock of water-fowl flying in a line, a peculiar shaped moon placed lower than the flying fowl—all com-

Screen (the second of the pair)

bined to produce a highly ornamental effect. (Fig. 9, 10)

It is essential for decorative pictures to have a certain air of detachment from the realities of nature to a certain extent. Things of beauty—flowers and birds, trees and waves—when painted true to nature are apt to excite in us a feeling of shock, surrounded as we are by a bewildering medley of the realities of life, and this prevents us from a full enjoyment of the beauty of the pictures. Too much separation from nature as in the geometrical patterns of straight lines and curves seen in Persian carpets, for instance, leaves an impression that there is something left unfinished, something to be desired. Some device has to be conceived of, by which the shape and color of things in nature are so changed as to look far more beautiful than the originals themselves.

There seem to be some rules regulating conventionalization in Japanese decorative painting. One of them governs the bold extraction of beauty apart from the entirety of nature. In the "Ryūo Shunsō Zu" which beautifully adorns the wall of the Chishakuin Temple, Kyōto, for instance, the thick trunk of a cherry-tree is only partially represented in the picture, the upper and lower portions having been left out. There are flower-loaded branches slanting toward the ground, but these are not connected with the trunk. In the "Setchū Ryūro Zu" by Sanraku, the same device has been used. Perhaps such license is not permitted by Western painters. Their method of procedure would be to reproduce a square space taken exactly from nature, in which a tree, be it a cherry-tree or a willow, occupies the focal point. The tree would be presented in its entirety, that is, with branches in their proper relation with the trunk. This is what the spirit of realism dictates.

The next thing to be noted is the fact that Japanese decorative painters have to arrange a number of slices taken from nature so as to produce a proportion, or a repetition that combines the whole picture into a thing of harmony. So much for explanation here. An inspection of the two masterpieces named above will make this point clearer than any words can do. Besides, the formal beauty that comes from proportion and repetition is what European esthetics deals with in a very systematic way.

The slices taken from nature are subjected to a simplifying process to a certain extent, their components undergoing geometrical configuration. The outlines of the pine needles in the " Matsu-Taka Zu " folding screens, which are depicted as a series of arcs, may be cited as an appropriate illustration. Simplification in the matter of color results in the reduction of all colors to one. Pine needles in nature have a variety of green colors, and also a variety of shading, but a realistic representation is a avoided and only one shade of green is adopted for the whole picture. Regarding the matter of coloring an additional remark should be made ; that is, for decorative effect truth to nature is often sacrificed. In the fold-

FIG. 11 Folding Screen showing Autumn Plants (Chishakuin Temple, Kyōto)

ing screen in question, it will be observed that a body of flowing water is shown in deep blue.

Simplification of form and color is also the basic formula in European esthetics, and it needs no elaboration in these pages. One more feature of Japanese decorative painting may be mentioned here. It is the practice to leave unpainted a part, sometimes quite a large part, of the bright ground of gold in a folding screen covered with gold-foil paper. The blank spaces occasionally contain geometrical arcs, technically called *kumo* or clouds. These " clouds " have some connection with *kasumi* (haze) which will be referred to in the next chapter. If the painting is on paper or silk, the space left unpainted is a white blank. Rationally such a white space should have something like a background scene painted on it. But the space is left blank from choice. To the mind of the Japanese artist, the blank space itself is decorative in effect, its ornamental value being equivalent to the gold color in the ground of folding-screen, the indigo-colored water, and pine-needles in deep green. The Japanese artist sees in the blank space, not something void of significance, but something that has an esthetic appeal. This traditional theory of the Japanese painter has to be taken into consideration by a Western student of Japanese decorative painting.

It should be noted that the decorative painting described above includes the works of the first-rate monochrome painters, such as Eitoku and Sanraku.

Their style shows a close adherence to the severe and stern features traditional to the monochrome painters. These paintings are no doubt masterpieces, but they lack elements of pleasurable excitement. They were chiefly intended for interior decoration in the Shogun's mansions. Some painted on a magnificent scale decorating the walls of the guests' chambers where formal audiences were held; others were intended for the decoration of sliding and folding screens in the sitting rooms of the Shogun or his wife. Naturally they would be expected to be impressive. Such decorative pictures would make fitting patterns for the " Nishijin " tapestry hung in the Palace of Peace at the Hague, but are unsuitable as models of art intended to enrich the daily lives of the people.

Painters of quieter pictures that suited the tastes of the people came to the fore in the Edo period (1615—1867). First to be mentioned is Kōetsu Honnami (1558—1637), then came Sōtatsu Tawaraya (? —1643), Kōrin Ogata (1663—1743), and Kenzan Ogata (1663—1743). These artists belonged to the class of ordinary townsmen. It was therefore natural that they should concern themselves more with peaceful and quiet beauty rather than with things that would inspire stern and severe feelings. Their works indicate that, though they were generally bold in their simplification of the forms in nature, the results, carried to the utmost extent, were free from effort and their beauty can be taken in at a glance. This may serve as an explanation of the esthetic principle of simplification as displayed in their pictures. Simplification of color is also carried to an extreme. Liberty in changing the colors of nature is such that the beholder often opens his eyes with astonishment.

The painter most typical of the period in this respect is Kōrin. His " Kaka Meiroku Zu " (Deer under a Tree in Bloom) and " Kōbai-Hakubai Zu Byōbu " (Folding-screen of Red and White Plum Blossoms ; see the illustration between p. 36 and p. 37) will readily impress one as far more simplified both in form and color than the decorative pictures by Eitoku and Sanraku in the Momoyama period. Especially in the case of Kōrin, it is generally acknowledged that simplified colors possess a peculiar attraction. His method of coloring is notably individual, and might be said to partake of the nature of industrial art.

It is usual in Japanese painting, as is the case with water-color painting in the West, to give color to pictures with pigments, mineral or vegetable in origin, dissolved in water. In pigments somewhat coarse in composition such as copper-green and indigo-blue, glue is sometimes added. But in this type of painting the coloring can never be so intense or persistent as in oil painting. Kōrin used a special technique, when painting cherry blossoms or chrysanthemums, for instance, which involved depositing white starch on the outlines of flowers and then giving them coloring—this is technically known as *moriage* (raising). Gold foil is made use of, too, in special cases. It is used in sprinkling and in painting some important lines, in which case the foil is dissolved in water to which glue has been added. One fact that is of no small interest to us concerning Kōrin and his contemporary painters of the same school is

FIG. 12 "Bateau-bridge" Ink-stone Box by Kōetsu
(National Museum of Tōkyō)

that they were not only painters of distinction, but also amateur industrial artists. Kōetsu, for instance, was the maker of an ink-stone box, named "Sano Funabashi" (Bateau-bridge) (Fig. 12), in which pieces of lead were inlaid to decorate the lacquer surface. The freedom in design noticeable in the piece is peculiarly his own. Kōrin also tried his hand at gold lacquer-ware, as may be seen by the ink-stone box, known as "Kakitsubata Yatsuhashi (Zig-zag Bridge and Iris) (Fig. 13). Kenzan was also skilled in the making of artistic pottery, on which he painted pictures of ornamental value. This fact is well known among collectors and lovers of art.

It appears that in the period under review the use of decorative pictures was not only on lacquerware and pottery, but also on all kinds of household goods for everyday use. Today, anyone who is a connoisseur of art can pick up in the curio shop or the stalls of pavement antique dealers things bearing such decorative pictures engraved, done in inlaid work, or cast in metals,—sword guards, *inro* (medicine-case), beads of tobacco-pouches, silver smoking-pipes, tortoise-shell combs and decorative hair-pins which are indispensable adjuncts in the coiffeur of Japanese women. Usually the motifs of these decorative pictures are flowers and birds. Just about this time there was popularity for the use of combinations of objects. The peony pairs with the lion, the plum-blossom with the *uguisu* (Japanese nightingale), the bamboo with the sparrow, the pine-tree with the

FIG. 13 Ink-stone Box with Zig-zag Bridge and Iris by Kōrin (National Museum of Tōkyō)

crane, waves with the *chidori* (plover), the willow with the swallow, and the maple-tree with the deer. These form only a partial list showing the principal objects usually paired together. Their combinations are still used by present-day craftsmen.

An interesting fact worth noting is that on the surfaces of *hanafuda* cards (used in a Japanese card game very popular with people of certain occupations and which seems to have had its origin in the period with which we are now concerned) pretty flowers and birds are painted for purposes of suited distinction and decoration. To describe some of these cards — in one there is a large moon rising peacefully over an autumn field, in another a wild boar standing in a *hagi* (bush-clover) bush, in another a curtain stretched among full-blooming cherry flowers ; another shows paulownia flowers of a luxuriant purple shade, and still another shows rain falling in a drizzle. This card game is banned in Japan as a gambling evil and beyond the pale of respectable society, but the cards are objects of art and are outstanding in artistic merit and the writer is tempted to advise the Westerner to have a look at some of the excellent specimens.

In concluding this topic, I wish to mention a painter of this school who is of great importance to Japanese young women. Strange to say, this artist is almost neglected by historians of Japanese painting. I mean Yūzen Umemaru, who had his workshop near the River Kamo in Kyōto and who was contemporaneous with Kōrin. Little is known of his life. The only definite thing known of him is that he went to the Luchoos and came back with a new method of dyeing which he acquired during his stay there. He worked with crêpe and silk on which were dyed decorative pictures of his own painting. The pictures or patterns dyed by his special method were of such bright beauty as to appeal strongly to the tastes of the common people. In popular appeal he was to be ranked much higher than Kōrin and others belonging to the same group. The gorgeous patterns now to be seen in the *kimono* of young Japanese ladies are mostly traceable in origin to the Kyōto painter and dyer. His works of art gained instantaneous and extensive vogue and without much exaggeration it may be said that *yuzen* materials were possessions regarded by damsels as next only to their lives. The *yuzen* patterns were later adapted in modern plants to the dyeing of cotton cloth and mousseline, and these commodities became so moderate in cost as to be well within the reach of the modest purse. Thus *yuzen* crêpe and *yuzen* mousseline have become household words in homes where there are young women in the family. Young womanfolk, especially *geisha* and dancers who wear beautiful *kimono*, with flowers strewn all over their figures, so to speak, owe a heavy debt of gratitude to Yūzen, though they are not aware of the fact, for his aid in helping them to full indulgence in the beautification of their persons. Should Yūzen come to life and learn of the

"Kachō Zu" (Hydrangea and a Pair of Fowls) by *Jakuchū Itō*

wide popularity of the patterns he invented, he would be highly delighted, notwithstanding the ingratitude of the fair sex so indebted to him.

III. PICTURE SCROLLS

A piece of paper, narrow and very long, on which are painted pictures of literary value or ones exemplifying a national tradition—such is a picture scroll (*emakimono*). When not in use, a picture scroll is rolled up and set aside for enjoyment in the future. The scrolls are often exhibited in museums opened out and in a long glass-case. Our readers may have had occasions to see such examples.

A picture scroll is perhaps without a counterpart in the West. Its origin is to be found in ancient Egypt. As an instance, one may point out the "Book of the Dead." Picture in this form existed in ancient China—in the Six-dynasty period (420—588). It is likely that Japan is indebted to China for the picture scroll, but the technique used in our picture scrolls is entirely Japanese, not borrowed from China as in the case of the monochrome painting, which genealogically belongs to the North-China school of painting. Hence the popular name of *Yamato-e*, or pure Japanese pictures.

The beginnings of *Yamato-e* were in the middle

of the Heian period (794—1185). The first painter of renown in this style of painting was Takayoshi Fujiwara (12th cent.). He used his own charming style in a pictorial representation of the " Genji Monogatari," a Japanese classical romance. The scroll has come down to us, though only in a fragment. " Genji Monogatari " is a novel of considerable length written by the most distinguished of our Heian bluestockings, Murasaki Shikibu (11th cent.). It ranks among the best in Japanese literature. In this romance is reproduced the atmosphere of the brilliant court life at the time of Genji-no-kimi, the hero, with a galaxy of talented ladies including Murasakino-ue.

The picture scroll of Takayoshi, which is an illustration of the novel—" Genji Monogatari Emaki," to give its full title—is most remarkable for its effective rendering of the elegant and romantic atmosphere of the court, the keynote of the " Genji Monogatari." But painting is an independent art, and no matter how skilfully the artist may interpret the atmosphere of the novel, if the picture itself has no merit, it is not worthy of much admiration. Viewed from this point, however, the scroll is a success. Human figures, houses, and flowers are outlined with fine lines, which are painted in pretty rich colors. Nothing tawdry, however, is to be found there—the colors are characterized by quietness and harmony. The details are put in moderation with fine, soft lines. Faces, for instance, are painted in

FIG. 14 "Chapter of Minori" from the "Genji

the *hikime-kagibana* method,—a line for the eye and a hook for the nose. The artist has succeeded in giving full expression to his conceptions in this simple way. The characters represented are natural in posture and exquisite in portrayal.

Let us study the *Minori* (sacred Law of Buddha), one of the chapters of the "Genji Monogatari" in the picture scroll mentioned above. (Fig. 14) The plot is as follows:—Murasaki-no-ue, with whom Genji-no-kimi is deeply in love, falls ill. Her illness hangs on and she gradually becomes worse, a fact

Monogatari " Picture Scroll by Takanobu Fujiwara

which is of great anxiety to Genji-no-kimi. Murasaki-no-ue, feeling that she has not long to live, is thinking of becoming a nun. To this intention her lover has no objection. The beauty of the flowers now blooming in glory in the garden will soon fade and similarly life, full of vicissitudes, will soon disappear like the morning dew. Genji-no-kimi also contemplates becoming a priest and places himself in the service of Buddha. Yet, as he is still young it requires no small amount of moral courage to renounce the attractions of the gay court life. He hesitates in his resolution to cut himself off from the affairs of the mundane world.

Spring has passed and summer comes on. The illness of Murasaki-no-ue increases in gravity. One day a *chūgū*, an affectionate friend, comes from the court to pay her a visit of sympathetic inquiry. She is pleased beyond measure, and, during a conversation which touches on a variety of topics, she reveals to her friend what she wishes to be done after she is gone. The *chūgū* is greatly affected and can hardly stop the tears that come welling up.

Summer is gone and the winds of autumn begin to blow, but the illness of Murasaki-no-ue still lingers on. She loses flesh, but this contrast with her former luxuriance of healthy beauty gives her a look of lofty nobility. The *chūgū* postpones her return to the court and continues to stay on with her sick friend. One windy evening, Genji-no-kimi makes his appearance at the house. Murasaki-no-ue tells him in a poem she improvizes that her passing away is near at hand. With his heart full of sorrow, he composes a poem in return saying that he is prepared to die with her. Murasaki-no-ue's condition suddenly becomes critical and she lays herself down at the foot of a tapestry screen. And thus she breathes her last.

It must be noted that in the picture scroll under review, the transition of scenes and the passage of time are indicated by words written in a beautiful hand and inserted between the pictures. In the picture scrolls of the Kamakura and Muromachi periods (1185—1568), such verbal indication of time and space is superseded by a pictorial device technically called *kasumi* (haze), of which more will be said in explanation later on.

The "Genji Monogatari Emaki" by Takayoshi Fujiwara served as a model for numerous painters of later generations who adopted the same theme for artistic expression. Another favorite theme for picture scroll artists is a biography of Michizane Sugawara (845—903), a scholar of distinction in the Heian period who stood so high in popular estimation that he was deified after his death. The shrine dedicated to his spirit is called Kitano Shrine or Temman-gū; and he is known as Tenjin-sama. He is the patron saint of learning and calligraphy. As a child I made early acquaintance with this divinity. In my primary school days, it was the practice of my mother to take me to a Temman-shrine to solicit for improvement in my scholarship. She also had my exercises in Chinese penmanship dedicated to the god.

The most noted of the scrolls dealing with Sugawara's life is the one called "Kitano Temman-gū Engi" by Nobuzane Fujiwara (1176—1268), a master in the Kamakura period. (Fig. 15) "Engi" means a historical account of a Shinto shrine or a Buddhist temple.

Nobuzane's scroll illustrates the chief incidents in the life of Sugawara, which are outlined below.

Michizane Sugawara was born of a family of

scholars. From this childhood his genius asserted itself in various ways. He distinguished himself especially in the study of ethics, politics, and literature. His accomplishments came to the notice of the Emperor, who appointed him to a position in his court. His profound learning and good character, to which was added a friendly love for mankind won for him the respect of many people and he was finally given the position of Minister of State. In this post he showed himself a fine statesman. He contributed much towards the administering of good government. Even such a great man was not without an enemy, however. Another holder of a portfolio, Tokihira Fujiwara by name, looked on Michizane with an eye

FIG. 15 Part of the "Kitano Temman-gū Engi"

(Kitano Shrine, Kyōto)

full of jealousy. He feared that, because of the brilliance of his illustrious colleague, he would suffer by contrast. So he was small enough to alienate the Imperial master against Michizane, whom he accused of being guilty of maladministration. His ruse was succeeded with the Emperor, and he ordered Michizane to be deported to Dazaifu in Kyūshū. This cruel treatment aroused no feeling of grievance in Michizane. His allegiance to his master was unshaken. In his exile he used to take out a suit of clothes given him by the Emperor as a prize for a splendid piece of poetry he had composed and offer a prayer for the welfare of the donor. It was also his habit to while away his time writing verses on the subject of an ancient plum-tree for which he had a special fondness. Thus the years rolled by while he lived a life of exile in the provincial town of Dazaifu. Finally he succumbed to illness and died without the forgiveness of the Emperor. Just at this time a sad thing happened in Kyōto. A storm raged in the Imperial capital and the Tokihira's mansion was struck by a thunderbolt and the master met a violent death. The tragedy was interpreted as a dispensation of Heaven. The Emperor realized for the first time the true facts of the case, and tried to make amends by bestowing a high court rank to Michizane posthumously. The courtiers co-operated with a number of citizens in carrying out a plan to erect a shrine in memory of the great scholar-statesman and his deeds of virtue.

FIG. 16 Part of the "Ippen Shōnin Gyōjō Ezu" (Priest Ippen's Life and Conduct in Picture)

This work of art by Nobuzane is bold in composition and replete with the charm of variety. There is a wealth of color in it, and great beauty is displayed in the quiet composed tone of the pictures.

A list of famous picture scrolls in Japan includes also productions representing the joint work of Yoshimitsu Tosa (14th cent.) and others—"Hōnen Shōnin Eden," "Ippen Shōnin Gyōjō Ezu," and "Shinran Shōnin Eden." (Fig. 16) These are pictorial biographies of famous Buddhist priests who founded the Japanese sects of Buddhism. Warriors in armor and on horseback engaged in battle was another theme which caught the fancy of the scroll painters. One of these, "Heiji Monogatari Emaki" by Keion Sumiyoshi (13th cent.), is counted among the masterpieces of its kind. (Fig. 17) A large num-

FIG. 18 Part of the

FIG. 19 Part of the

"Kokawa-dera Engi"

"Ishiyama-dera Engi"

ber of these scrolls are in the possession of the Boston Museum of Art, and some of the readers of this booklet may had an opportunity to inspect them. Some picture scrolls depict the histories of Buddhist temples, and good work can be found among them. As they are connected with the faith and folklore of the nation, they may be of interest to visitors from overseas. A few will be discussed briefly below.

The first to be mentioned is " Kokawa-dera Engi " of unknown authorship. (Fig. 18) The story the scrolls illustrate is as follows. In the country-side of Nara, there was a wealthy person named Sadayū. He had a daughter. She fell ill one day, and the medicine she took did her no good. She grew worse day by day and her condition became so critical that it was feared she might not survive another day. Sadayū and the whole family were overcome by deep sorrow, when a friar, a stranger to the place, came to the door of the patient's home. He stayed overnight in the house and prayed to Buddha for the recovery of the daughter. His prayer was answered and miraculously the maiden was cured instantly. The father offered him valuable treasure as a token of gratitude. The offer was declined, but in place of the treasure, he asked for one of the daughter's *kimonos*. This he obtained, and, before taking his departure, he gave a fragmentary bit of information about himself saying that he was one lived at Kokawa near Wakayama. Sadayū journeyed all the way to Kokawa to try and satisfy his sense of indebtedness by doing something for his benefactor. But the friar was nowhere to be found. At last Sadayū made his way to a small temple in the heart of the mountains, and there he asked for a night's lodging. All of a sudden he caught sight of the figure of Senju Kannon, the one-thousand-handed goddess of mercy to whom the temple was dedicated—and lo and behold!—he saw his daughter's garment which the priest had carried away with him, hanging from the image of the Kannon. He perceived at once that the priest was really this Kannon, temporarily disguised as a friar. He spent all his fortune in the erection of a splendid temple for the enshrinement of the Kannon. This is how the Kokawa-dera Temple was brought into being. Sadayū became a priest, and spent all the rest of his days in the service of the Kannon.

The painter of the " Ishiyama-dera Engi " is also not known. (Fig. 19) This is the story it tells. Once upon a time a government official in an eastern province of Japan came up to the capital—then Kyōto—in connection with a law suit. He won his case, and arranged to send his servant back to his country home, entrusting him with the written judgment. He was to follow him sometime later. As he was crossing the bridge over the River Seta, the servant carelessly dropped the document he carried with him into the river. He made a thorough search for the paper but all in vain. As a last resort, he made his way to the Ishiyama Temple not far distant in search of help. There he prayed to Kannon for assistance in the recovery of the lost paper. That night Kannon appeared to him in a dream, and told him where he would find the document in question. Following the instructions, he angled for carp in the River Uji the following day. Just as Kannon had told him, he found the lost article in a carp he hooked. People marvelled at this further instance of a ready response to a prayer to the goddess Kannon.

The story graphically told by the " Seigan-ji Engi " by Yukimitsu Tosa (14th cent.) is outlined below. Long, long ago, there was in a certain place a sculptor named Kemmonshi. In order to improve in skill, he crossed over to China, and, because of his ability which was of no mean order, he soon distinguished himself as a master of the art. He was taken into the service of the Emperor. His success was so signal that he was given a fine residence with a Chinese beauty for his wife. Not long after, a lovely son was born to them. Amidst this life of happiness and prosperity, the thought of his home country came to him and he became homesick. Determined to go back to Japan, he applied to his Imperial master for permission. But his ardent request was not granted, and the Emperor put a ban on the sailings of Chinese ships to Japan fearing lest the sculptor should take passage to Japan in secret. Kemmonshi was at a loss over what to do. His homesickness could not be suppressed. Then it was that a capital idea flashed

Part of the "Nezame Monogatari" (A picture scroll)
(Collection of Mrs. S. Hara, Yokohama)

There are two types of picture scrolls. One is the linear kind which depicts tersely the development of a story with a free use of fluent lines: it is quite vivid in movement and expression. The other is highly decorative, with a rich pigmentation. The picture shown above is a fine specimen of the latter, the flower of the aristocracy in the Heian period (794-1186).

upon his mind. Confining himself to his studio, he began to carve a large bird, which was successfully completed in due course. The remarkable thing about this bird was that it was designed to make aerial flights. It was a sort of airplane. On this bird-plane, he started off for his homeland, leaving behind him a chisel as a reminder to his son. A number of years elapsed after his departure, and the child grew into a youth, no less talented than his father in the art of sculpture. The chisel his father had left as a memento constantly reminded him of his dear father, whom he longed to see. He sailed by ship to Japan. Being a stranger in a strange land, he had to undergo many vicissitudes during his travels in search of his father, but at last he succeeded in finding him at Nara, where he was working as a sculptor in the shrine of Kasuga. Attributing their reunion to the benevolent assistance of Buddha, the father and son co-operated in the production of an image of Amida (*Amitabha Buddha*). In this task they had the co-operation of Kannon and Seiji-Bosatsu (*Mahasthamaprapta*), who carved wood and whetted the chisels for them in the workshop. As might be expected, the statue they made was of exquisite workmanship. It gained the honor of being chosen as the main icon of the Seiganji Temple.

The scene of the story told by the pictures in Yu-kihiro Tosa's "Yūzū Nembutsu Engi" (15th cent.) is laid in the Mibu-dera Temple in a suburb of Kyōto. There lived in olden days a priest named

Ryōnin. His fast place of study was on Mt. Hiei, where he was noted for the beauty of his voice. When he was reciting a sutra, even the birds were facinated by his charming voice. He was versed in the art of *shōmyō*, which is Buddhistic vocal music. For some reason, however, he was expelled from the mountain temple when he was twenty-three years old. This event marked the beginning of the period of his real scholastic pursuits. He settled down in the Mibu-dera Temple and there he founded a Buddhist denomination called "Yū ū Nembutsu." *Nembutsu* means the utterance of the name of Buddha, and it was believed that by virtue of a constant repetition of the utterance one could enjoy life in the Buddhist Paradise after death. The Jōdo and Shinshū sects, which today boast a vast number of believers, are branches of this Nembutsu sect. Ryōnin introduced a modification in the practice of uttering Buddha's name. He decreed that *nembutsu* is more effective when, instead of being uttered by a solitary voice, it is said in chorus by a large number of persons. This is the summary of the story pictorially told in the scroll.

These scrolls deal with narratives, which naturally involve the shifting of scenes and the passage of time. In the early period of picture scrolls, "Genji Monogatari Emaki" for instance, those changes of scene and time were indicated by writing inserted to show continuity, but as has already been mentioned, a device technically styled as *kasumi* came to

FIG. 20 Part of the "Kitano Temman-gū Engi"—an example showing the use of *kasumi*

FIG. 21 Part of the "Kasuga Gongen Reigenki"—an example of *fukinuki-yatai*

be used later. The *kasumi* is a technique peculiar to the *Yamato* school of painting.

Kasumi or haze is an atmospheric phenomenon, allied to mist and fog. To the Japanese mind, however, this haze is felt to be quite distinct from them. On a calm day, when the air is different in density each layer forms a stratum stretching to a great length, and moisture borne by those strata covers the sky in long horizontal sweeps. This is what is called *kasumi*. In poetry, both in *waka* and *haiku*, the phenomenon is treated as a thing characteristic of the spring season. *Kasumi* is to be seen at twilight in spring, forming a number of milk-white streaks at the foot of a mountain, for instance. This type of scenery is rich in esthetic flavor.

The *kasumi*, a characteristic feature in scroll painting, consists of a pattern with several streaks of considerable length. Sometimes it has a beautiful bend describing a semi-circle. A word of explanation as to the symbolism of the *kasumi*. Suppose a priest of lofty character is taking a walk in the mountains. In a scroll picture there may be pictured as a setting groups of trees with luxuriant foliage on both sides of the priest and there may be a half moon in the sky. The whole atmosphere is that of solitude. The scene may be intersected by white *kasumi* forming slender streaks, introducing the next scene, in which there is, for instance, a hamlet with seven or eight cottages scattered about. Here the priest is surrounded by a dozen good people of the village, who make a contribution of a penny in return for a piece of paper containing a picture from the brush of the recluse. Cocks crow and dogs run about. Another *kasumi* curtain, and another scene is ushered in. It has for its background the Imperial court at Kyōto. It is understood that there was an interval of several years between this and the preceding scene. The priest is represented as being given a high court rank, and there are a number of courtiers offering him words of congratulation. Such is the typical use of *kasumi*.

It appears that there are few instances in Western schools of painting where scenes varying in time and location, are put in one picture. It is not fair to judge the merit of the picture scroll by this standard alone. In fact, a combination of scenes differing in time and location does exist in European pictures. The " Deliverance of St. Peter " by Raphael seen in one of the rooms of the Vatican is a case in point. The fresco contains in a semicircular space three scenes arranged in succession and differing in time. At the left armed Roman soldiers are on guard at the entrance steps to the prison where St. Peter is incarcerated. By the providence of God, they are fast asleep. The middle scene shows a prison cell where angels wrapped in the radiance of glory have come up the steps and are removing the chain from the sacred prisoner. At the right is St. Peter being led out of the prison by the angels. In this instance from Raphael, the disparity of time and place is marked by substantial pillars, while in the case of the picture-scroll painter the *kasumi* serves the same purpose.

The *kasumi* was an invention mothered by the necessity of meeting the requirements of a story as told on a scroll, but it came to be used even in pictures that had no story to tell. In painting a picture on folding screens, for instance, the artists of the *Yamato* school frequently resorted to this device. There the *kasumi* is ornamental than useful, taking the place of the cloud, a succession of semicircular figures, to be seen in the decorative pictures of Sanraku Kanō.

There are other things besides the *kasumi* used in the technique of the picture-scroll painters. The device of *fukinuki-yatai*, or roofless houses, for instance, is already used in the "Genji Monogatari Emaki" and the "Temman-gū Engi." By the method the people in a house are seen obliquely from above as the roof and the ceiling are removed so as to make them visible. (Fig. 21) There is no denying the fact that this is unrealistic and unnatural, but it must be admitted that in art some degree of unnaturalness should be allowed as license, or even welcomed, as it sometimes aids in the enhancement of the artistic merits. If realism is strictly followed, and a picture is made so that the interior of the house is seen from the garden, the figures and furniture would become so complicated that the clearness of the actions of the people would be interfered with. Walls and sliding screens would also shut out the view. The reader is reminded in this connection of the method used in stagecraft in which the "fourth wall," to use the words of Ibsen, is always removed. So a room on the stage is, in most cases, without a roof or a ceiling, only the portions of such as would be visible from the audience being nailed on as if by way of apology. The idea of *fukinuki-yatai* may be comprehended if one would consider that the house in the picture is something like a house on the stage looked at by spectators from their seats on the fourth or fifth floor.

The *yūdō-shiki*, a term for convenience meaning shifting system, is another of the *Yamato*-picture devices peculiar to picture-scroll painting. By *yūdō-shiki* I mean that the view-point of an onlooker, instead of being fixed at one place, shifts constantly from one point to another. This is a feature almost unknown in Western painting, and the foreigner may think it strange when he sees it for the first time. This is a trick frequently used when the main character in the picture takes a stroll through varying scenes of nature—from mountain to village and from village to ravine, from ravine to town. In such cases, winding is purposely made in the route over which he travels, so that each bend may conveniently present the characteristic feature of the surrounding natural scenery. It is inevitable that, objectively considered, the combination becomes unrealistic. As an extreme example, a temple, which is rectangular or square in shape is distorted on purpose, and, while rationally only two sides of the building should be visible at a time, the front and two other sides are shown at the same time so that the architectural design on those sides may be recognized. The sides, therefore, are represented somewhat like two wings. This deviation from realism must be looked upon as a device specially designed to meet the requirements of picture composition.

Another peculiarity of picture-scroll painting may be mentioned here. That is its disregard or distortion of the relative size of an object with distance. The parallel of a desk or a room, for instance, almost invariably widens as it runs into the background. No satisfactory explanation has ever been made about this irrational treatment. In the *Yamato* pictures this tradition is faithfully followed in almost every case. To the Japanese mind the distortion of the size of a desk or of a room in its relationship to distance has the advantage of emphasizing its existence. It is a case of contrary psychological effect. It might be argued that adherence to reality would fail to arrest the attention of the spectator because of the inconspicuousness that comes from naturalness.

The relative size of objects is also often disregarded, instances being by no means rare in picture scrolls. A word of some justification may be said. In the picture of a person sitting inside a house, the very fact that the latter contains the former makes it larger than the content. But when a person stands outside a house, the house need not be larger than the person. An unfriendly critic may say, with justice, that it is no more than a bit of idealism observable in the pictures of children and of uncivilized people. A picture scroll has for its primary aim the illustration of a story, and as man is more important than objects, therefore the size of the house is immaterial. It must not be overlooked that such idealism carried with it an esthetic effect. By purposely giving small proportions to the house, which otherwise would occupy an unwieldly large space, the picture is braced and in its way exhibits the beauty of symmetry.

In art unexpected results are often produced, and this is a truth that should not be lost sight of.

IV. UNREALISM IN JAPANESE PAINTING

Realism is not non-existent in Japanese arts.
As an evidence one may cite the instance of " Jū
Dai Deshi " (Ten Great Disciples of the Buddha),
a group of sculpture produced in the Nara period
(645—794), more than one thousand years ago. (Fig.
22) This group of figures in life size is so realistic
in the proportions of the parts of the body, bone
structure, and sinews—so true to anatomical facts
that one feels that there is scarecely anything left
to be desired. Pieces of sculpture by Unkei (13th
cent.) and Kaikei (13th cent.) in the Kamakura
period (1185—1392), such as the " Niō-zō," statues
of Niō (*Vajrapani*), the twin guardians of Buddhism,
for instance, belong in the same category. (Fig. 24,
25) These giants who function as guardians of the
gates of a Buddhist temple, though exaggerated in
structure and sinews, are so realistically represented
that no one looking at them can gainsay the fact.
What I mean by " realistically represented " is that
the human figure or an object is shown as it is, as
it appears to the artist.   It refers, of course, to the

FIG. 22 One of the "Ten Great Disciples of Buddha"
(Kōfukuji Temple, Nara)
In its realistic attainment this compares favorably
with the later masterpiece by Kaikei (Fig. 23)

FIG. 23 One of the "Ten Great Disciples of Buddha"
by Kaikei   (Daihōonji Temⲣle, Kyōto)

FIG. 24 Statue of Niō (the tight-mouthed) by Unkei and Kaikei
(Tōdaiji Temple, Nara)

FIG. 25 Statue of Niō (the open-mouthed) by Unkei and Kaikei
(Tōdaiji Temple, Nara)

expression, not the theme, that is, whether a human figure or an object is or is not a product of the imagination of the creator.

In Japan realism was an attribute of sculpture, not of painting. In painting, whether it be monochromes, picture scrolls, decorative pictures, *Nanga* school pictures, or color prints, realism is conspicuously non-existent. How is that to be accounted for? It is true there were some Japanese painters who were called realists and painted pictures which, viewed in parts, make one feel almost they are realistic. These painters were represented by Ōkyo Maruyama (1733—1795) and others of the same school, who flourished in the middle of the Edo period (1615—1867). Ōkyo's " Shōsetsu Zu Byōbu " (Folding Screen of Snow-covered Pine-trees) has the crooked trunk of an old pine-tree that gives an impression of roundness, and branches and clusters of needles that are faithfully executed, together with a kind of shading used in painting that impress one with the fact that the artist aimed at being true to nature. (Fig. 26) But his realism is strictly combined to parts, and viewed in its entirety, the picture is a production far removed from realism in the Western sense ; it is after all a products of Japanese tradition. (Pl. 7)

In the unrealism of Japanese painting, three points may be mentioned for special consideration. One is the absence of the background. This is a feature almost universal in Japanese painting in all its

branches. Needless to say, the background is essential in showing the location or the setting of an
object painted, or, in the case of a human figure,
the process of time in relation to an event. There
can be no person or thing that is independent of
time and space. But Japanese pictures lack this essential. In the case of the "Shōsetsu Zu" referred
to above, the background is lacking. No one can
tell whether the pine is growing on the beach, locat-
ed on a mountain top, or transplanted to a garden
for its beauty of branch arrangement.

It is a tradition that such a pine-tree is made
independent of its location, whether it be the beach,
a mountain top, or a garden. The pine-tree itself
is the thing aimed at. The mind of the artist is fo-
cused on the pine-tree; all else is blurred. This

～ 85

might be the correct view of such an idealism, but it appears that there may be another more cogent reason for it. It is this. In Japanese painting there is no background, that part being left blank. This, in the case of decorative painting, may be accounted for by the exigency of simplifying the picture by the elimination of trifling details, as has already been mentioned. Another way of thinking is that the substitution of the background with a blank space carries with it a symbolic meaning.

As the reader may be aware, Eugène Carrière, the nineteenth century French master, had the habit of painting his backgrounds all in sepia. But this sepia makes one feel that in its monotony there are a variety of things moving about. Take his " Maternity " as an example. The picture has in the foreground only a mother and her two children. This is all the picture contains, excepting a few pieces of furniture and some picture frames dimly visible in the background. This was Carrière's customary method; hence one talks of him as an interpreter of a dream-like art. There is something resembling this in Japanese painting. The difference is that in Japanese painting blank space takes the place of the sepia patch. To the Japanese mind the blank space has some symbolic value. In the " Shōsetsu Zu," for instance, it may stand for the waves of the sea ; or for a chain of mountains viewed from a mountain top; or for a wide expanse of lawn in a garden. This is what I call symbolic. A Western appreciator of Japanese painting is advised to bear in mind that the painter was conscious of this symbolic value of blank space—the eloquence of silence.

The second point that makes Japanese paintings unrealistic is that they lack perspective. In desks and rooms painted in scroll-pictures perspective of the objects is entirely disregarded or reversed as has already been mentioned, and an explanation bearing on the matter, though brief, has been given. In landscapes where scenes from nature are treated, almost equal unconcern is shown for perspective. In European paintings perspective forms an important factor in bringing out the beauty of a picture, and there is ample justification for giving it such importance. Is the Japanese painter unconscious of the beauty that comes from observing the rule of perspective?

I must frankly state that this was the case with the Japanese painters of the past. In Europe landscapes formed an independent branch of painting in the 17th and 18th centuries. In so far as perspective is concerned, the Japanese painters in earlier centuries were very backward in progress. In them the study of the scientific and optical aspects of painting was lacking. Whether they were monochrome painters of the *Hokuga* school or amateur artists of the *Nanga* school, they painted imaginary landscapes according to the " San-en-no-hō " (method of three distances), which was introduced from China. " San-en-no-hō " means a method by which the features of a landscape, whether it be an extensive field, or a high mountain, or a deep ravine, are made to look far away. To make a view look distant is what it teaches, and to make one look near is disregarded. It is true that care is taken so that, in comparing the pine and other trees, for instance, that are painted in the foreground, the plain, the mountain, and the ravine look far off. But in such a case, no consideration is given to the proper relative distance of the group in the background and that in the foreground. The same may be said of the relationship between a village or a river-side district with a sprinkling of cottages painted in the foreground and the mountains towering in the distance.

It is undeniable that in the production of the later Edo period (1615—1867), such, for instance, as Hokusai Katsushika's "Fugaku Sanjūrokkei," (Thirty-six Views of Mt. Fuji) and Hiroshige Andō's "Tōkaidō Gojūsan-tsugi" (Fifty-three Stages on the Tōkaidō), the sense of distance is fairly well brought out, as the nature of the pictures required a greater approach to reality. (See the last chapter.) But these are true landscapes and do not belong to the class of pictures in which the scenes from nature took shape in the imagination of the painter. We are here concerned with imaginary landscapes (*sansui-ga*). There are also in the latter part of the Edo period some pictures in which the painters seemed to have delighted in bringing out the sense of distance by the adoption of the European law of perspective. Their knowledge of the law of perspective was so imperfect that in some pictures, Masanobu Okumura's " Shibai-goya Zu " (Picture of a Theater) (Fig. 27) and Shigenaga Nishimura's " Tsukimi-za-shiki Zu " (Picture of a Moon-viewing Party) (Fig. 28), for instance, the law was not faithfully followed all round, its violation being shown in parts. To these matters no further consideration will be given here.

Regarding the method adopted by Japanese painters in their imaginary landscapes—the pushing of all things into the distance and flattening them, with a complete disregard of the sense of distance—the following explanation may be appropriate. The pictures, as has already been said, are imaginary ones

FIG. 27 "Picture of a Theater" by Masanobu Okumura
(National Museum of Tōkyō)

~ 89

FIG. 28 "Picture of a Moon-viewing Party" by Shigenaga
Nishimura   (National Museum of Tōkyō)

and at the same time they are pictures intended for
decoration. It is perhaps more accurate to say that
they are made decorative because of their being imaginary pictures. As is well known, the third di-
mension is done away with in all decorative pictures,
presumably to meet the requirement of esthetic simplification.

For instance, when a person stands in a garden
one day in late spring and feasts his eyes absently
on the beauty of trees, he has a feeling that is dream-
like in its fascination. In such a state of mind, all
things in his vision become flattened, the sense of
distance been lost. The roses, peonies, and lilies
directly before him or the *shii* (pasania) and *kashi*
(oak) looming in the distance all are reduced on the

same level, either lifted up or sunk down as the case may be. My idea is that a picture becomes purely decorative when the painter sees the landscape lifted up on the same level in the foreground. When the landscapes is seen on the same level in the background, the picture becomes one painted according to the law of " San-en " mentioned above. To the question, " Why is there no perspective in Japanese pictures ? ", the only possible answer seems to be that the painters, influenced by the flight of imagination, had reached a state of intoxication.

I now come to the third evidence. That is, Japanese pictures lack shading. This is a characteristic of Japanese painting, serving as another proof that it is not realistic. The rotundity of an object, as has been said, can be shown by means of the brush-line alone, without the aid of shading. However, every object has phases of light and shade ; it must also have a shadow falling on other objects. Why have these facts been disregarded by the Japanese painter ?

The answer is that the painter aims at heightening the decorative effect by a simplification of the painting process. From a personal point of view I should like to make this additional remark : that this question is somehow connected with the latitude in which Japan is situated and the architectural peculiarity of the Japanese house influenced by the geographical situation of the country. Let us examine the 17th-century Dutch pictures showing domestic interiors; for example, Adrian van Ostade's "A Painter in his Atelier" or Peter de Hooch's "A Woman Reading a Book." In a country situated in a high latitude, the dim light shining in obliquely through the window is valued a precious blessing and this fact, as one might readily perceive, makes the inhabitant of such a country extremely sensitive to the shade produced by the dim light. This plainly accounts in part for the minute realism which characterizes the paintings of the Netherlands and Flanders. Compared with these paintings, those of Italy, with its warm climate and orange trees flowering in luxuriance, even the pictures of the Renaissance masters, lack such minuteness of shading.

Generally speaking, Japan being more southern in its latitude than Italy, is almost always flooded with light. It would not be surprising, if the Japanese painter were more apathetic to shading, Besides, temperature and humidity have let the people to adopt a type of construction in architecture that is extremely airy. Between the pillars in the walls there are earthen sections, but very often *shōji* and *fusuma*, sliding paper-screens are used. These screens are usually slided off, so that the rooms overflow with light. In some rooms the light flows in from the south and the east or from the south and the west, and in others from three directions—south, east, and west. The contents of a room, whether human figures or furniture, cast scarcely any shadows. If they do, the shadows are too faint to attract notice.

These facts of natural environment and methods of living may serve as an explanation of why Japanese pictures have no shading.

As is known to the initiated, the French impressionists, whose main aim in painting is the portrayal of light, have taken considerable suggestion from Japanese pictures, especially from the color prints (*ukiyo-e*). Vincent van Gogh, that genius of the post-impressionist school, uses no shading whatever in his pictures. Light effects alone very often form the theme of his paintings. So with Paul Gauguin, and also Henri Matisse, our contemporary master, and Pablo Picasso in his productions of a certain period.

In the preceding paragraphs, three evidences have been given in support of the assertion that Japanese pictures lack elements of realism. However, there was a school of artists who may be said to be fully realistic in these three respects. That school is represented by Kōkan Shiba (1747-1818) and Denzen

FIG. 29 " Ferrying at the River Ōi " by *Kōkan Shiba*
(Academy of Fine Arts, Tōkyō)

FIG. 30 "Mt. Asama" by Denzen Aōdō

(National Museum of Tōkyō)

Aōdō (1747-1822), pioneers of Western-style painting in Japan. These men studied it at Nagasaki, the only Japanese port then open to foreign intercourse, and painted pictures in a scientific and realistic way, using imported Dutch pictures for models. Their pictures are chiefly landscapes, though there are some portraits among them. In these pictures there are background, perspective, and shading. Kōkan's "Ō-igawa Zu" (Ferrying at the River Ōi) (Fig. 29) and Denzen's "Asamayama Zu" (Mt. Asama) (Fig. 30) may be mentioned as examples possessing considerable merit.

However, the period during which these men flourished was sadly lacking in artists' implements and material, and naturally these pioneers were much handicapped in their work of introducing the Western style of painting. It was after the Restoration of Meiji (1868) that oil painting began to develop in this country. Especially phenomenal was

94 ～

its progress in the closing years of the Meiji era (1868-1912), when the methods of the French impressionists were transplanted here. The past two or three decades have witnessed a great activity among the young Japanese painters who drew inspiration from all the main movements in art, especially painting, introduced from the West a few years after their initiation and subsequent to the rise of impressionism. The reader may have had the opportunity of seeing specimens of this sort in art galleries, exhibitions, or art stores.

V. ARTISTIC FEATURES OF *TOKONOMA*

In Japanese houses the important rooms invariably have a *tokonoma*. A *tokonoma* is a kind of alcove raised 4 or 5 inches higher than the matted floor. For its pillar and the sill costly materials of high decorative value are used—for instance, a log of polished maple or red pine or a bamboo trunk turned a beautiful purple after being exposed to smoke for a couple of centuries. In the Japanese home the *tokonoma* is a place of honor. Here a *kakemono*, a picture mounted on a hanging scroll, is hung up, and here objects of art are displayed for the admiration of the visitor and for the enjoyment of the members of the household.

Opinions are divided as to the origin of the *tokonoma*. The most reliable one is probably this: it was first used as a place in which to hang a Buddhist picture and to hold a stand on which gifts to Buddha could be placed. Today, however, such religious associations are entirely gone, and the reasons for the *tokonoma* now are purely artistic. Hence its decoration with specially valuable wood chosen with as great care as the gilt frames for oil paintings and the setting for the stage in Western countries. All of which have this quality in common, that the things they enclose are not scenes from real life, but from the imaginary world of art.

It follows then that we can presume the hanging picture on show in the *tokonoma*, whether it be a

Tokonoma with a hanging picture and *ikebana*

monochrome landscape or a historic picture of the *Yamato* school or a decorative picture of flowers or birds, to be a thing of art. The picture itself is enclosed in tasteful old tapestry, just as an oil painting is framed in good wood. A detailed account will be made later of the mounting of a hanging picture, so mention will not be made here. Suffice it to say that careful mounting constitutes an art in itself, from the necessity to make it in keeping with the nature of the picture and to set off its beauty. This is easily understood when the reader reflects on the function of the frame in European paintings.

From the preceding it may be gathered that a Japanese hanging picture is put at its best advantage when placed in the *tokonoma*. A production of artistic distinction, so placed, dominates not only the *tokonoma* but also the entire room. If the picture is a monochrome which is severe in tone, the people looking at it will feel restrained. If it is an elegant picture of the *Yamato* school, they will feel exhilarated. The effect is a pleasurable one when the *tokonoma* picture is a decorative one representing flowers and birds. Pictures done by mediocre artists fail to exert such an influence. Perhaps it may be said that hanging a picture in the *tokonoma* is the best way of testing its merits.

So precious are such hanging pictures to their owners that they are usually rolled up, kept in boxes specially provided for them, and only taken out for exhibition when the occasion is appropriate. Ceremonial occasions and the advent of a new season are considered appropriate times for making changes in the hanging pictures. The New Year season is definitely such an occasion, and pictures of auspicious association, such as the figure of Jurōjin, symbolic of longevity, or those representing pine-trees and the crane, a combination suggestive also of long life, are selected. When, one remembers that in Japanese homes the New Year holidays are observed with great ceremony, it will be readily understood that monochromes on account of their sober and severe tone are considered to be more suitable to the spirit of the season. In March, the season of the Doll Festival which gives innocent enjoyment to all Japanese girls, the hanging pictures chosen will naturally be elegant ones of the *Yamato* school, such as those dealing with feminine charms, perhaps Murasaki Shikibu (a literary court lady of 11th century) viewing the moon, or young girls picking edible herbs in spring. In May, the season of the Boys' Festival, the pictures become more masculine in character in hopes that the young boys will grow up to a vigorous and happy manhood. There will perhaps be pictures of Shōki, famed in Chinese tradition for his victorious combat over the devils or of the carp which are popularly believed to leap over waterfalls in their progress upstream. Between these red-letter days, the *tokonoma* is not left without a hanging picture, for a *tokonoma* minus a hanging picture is like the play of Hamlet with the hero left out. The master of the house takes care to have some picture appropriate to the season hung up at all times. In the height of summer, the picture should be one suggestive of pleasant coolness—lotus flowers with their jewelled water drops on the leaves, a water-wheel on the River Yodo, or a chaste woman with her long hair freshly washed and cleaned. The autumn suggests its own congenial pictures. These would be pictures of the autumnal tints on Mt. Takao or of those autumnal flowers—*kikyō* (a kind of bell flower) and *karukaya* (a kind of miscanthus), for instance. One can easily see that a Japanese home must be provided with a rich store of hanging pictures, fourteen or fifteen at least. When these hanging scrolls include several showing calligraphic inscriptions which are regarded by both Japanese and Chinese experts as representative of a fine branch of art, the number may be smaller. But if, however, these autographs are stanzas from Chinese poetry indicative of the seasons, there must be a good supply of them so that the scroll hung up may be in happy harmony with the time of the year.

The *tokonoma* is not entirely devoted to the display of a *kakemono*. On the floor there must be a stand tastefully made of *shitan* (red sandal-wood) or maple on which is placed some object of ornamental value. Usually it is a few flowers arranged decoratively in a heavy bronze vase, an elegant porcelain basin or a simple vessel made of a piece of bamboo-stem.

Ikebana, or floral composition, is said to be Buddhistic in origin, but the religious sentiment is lost in the art as practised at present, it being chiefly esthetic in purpose now. It is for this reason that floral composition is considered a special form of art. This decorative art was introduced from China during the middle of the Muromachi period (1392-1568) down to the opening years of the Edo period (1615-1867). It appears that this art was fairly popular in the Ming and Ch'ing dynasties in China (1368-1911), though today it is not practised in that ancient land. In Japan, on the contrary, it has continued in popularity and today there exist thirty or forty branches of the art. *Ikebana* is practised in almost all the homes throughout the country. There are a few other special arts which are allied to floral composition, one of which is *chanoyu*, or ceremonial tea.

Since *chanoyu* or ceremonial tea, is quite closely connected with the other fine arts in Japan, a word here about it would not be out of place. But, as there is a volume in this series that treats of the subject, I shall refrain from going into it.

Floral composition, viewed from an esthetic standpoint, may be classified under two headings—one which is based on line and one which is based on color. The latter is most fittingly represented by *moribana* which may be described as a school of floral composition which was created in the middle of the Meiji era (1868-1912). This school attempted to show to the best advantage the different tone of colors in the flowers imported from Europe and America, such as dahlias, tulips, marguerites, and carnations. However, in *moribana* the flowers used are not confined to foreign and exotic ones only since such Japanese flowers as tree-peonies, camellias, and Kerrias (Japan globeflower) are also used, but there is this peculiarity in the treatment of all these flowers. The stalks are cut short, so that the beauty of the flowers themselves is emphasized for the appreciation of the observer. Perhaps it is because of this that the flowers are usually arranged in flat vessels. In Japanese houses, *moribana* arrangements are chiefly used for the decoration of the *tokonoma*, and accordingly care is taken to place them so that they look prettiest when viewed from the parlor. But lately *moribana* arrangements are being used in hotels and restaurants for table decoration, and, to suit the changed circumstances, care is taken to make the group look attractive to a viewer from any angle.

In contrast with *moribana*, the original floral composition uses lines as its keynote. In this school, the pine-tree, the plum-tree, the *hagi* (*Lespedeza*), the orchid, etc. are used by preference, as these plants have something characteristic in their stems, branches, stalks and leaves that interest the composers. These features of interest are all based on the beauty of lines—lines that are thick and strong, lines that are vigorous and suggestive of speed, or lines that are fine and flexible, describing the same arc. When these plants are used in arrangements the stems and branches are never cut short. They are bent by hand in various ways to suit the artist as he works. The bending is technically described by a variety of antiquated terms of the art, but it is in reality very similar to composition in painting. The Westerner looking at a floral composition should think of it as a plant in a Japanese picture—a monochrome, a decorative pictures, or a painting of the *Nanga* school.

As a matter of fact, in the floral compositions ornamenting the *tokonoma* there are those suggestive of monochromes with their severe and chaste lines, those reduced to such simplified geometrical lines as in gorgeous decorative pictures, or those as gentle in touch as the pictures of the *Nanga* school of which farther mention will be made later. This difference in style seems to come from differences in the various schools. No mention needs to be made of the fact that though the lines form the basic features of a floral composition, the beauty of the color of the leaves and flowers, as in the case of paintings, adds to its attractiveness. As has been said before, the hanging scroll and the floral composition should be in happy harmony when used as decorations for the *tokonoma*. This is partly because there is some resemblance between floral compositions, as objects of pleasure to the eye, and Japanese paintings. When the themes of the picture hung in the *tokonoma* is renunciation of the world, as in "Kanzan Jittoku," already mentioned above, a gay floral composition such as a tree-peony, for instance, would be inappropriate, as the flower of a tree-peony is symbolic of wealth. A floral composition that would be in accord with the picture might contain *ran* (orchids) with its subtle fragrance, or, according to the season, *karasu-uri* (snake gourd) or *akebi* (*Akebia quinata*) which have a rustic beauty. Even *bonsai*—a diminutive pine-tree in a pot, for instance—would be more fitting.

The raising of *bonsai* is another art peculiar to Japan. *Bonsai*, unlike a floral composition, in which only cut flowers are arranged in vases, consists of the whole plant, roots and all. The pots used are usually flat and the trees—both deciduous and evergreen—are planted carefully in them. The pot is usually a convenient size for placing in the *tokonoma*. This restricts the height of the tree in it to one foot at the tallest. The trees are transplanted when very young and stunted in their growth by a process known only to the cultivators. Sometimes, however, naturally dwarfed trees found on cliffs of high mountains are collected for potting. These plants are more highly appreciated by *bonsai* lovers because they lack artificiality, having been nurtured by nature. A potted tree is considered ideal when suggests the solitude of a mountain recess. Such a plant, if available, would make a very happy combination with the hanging picture, " Kanzan Jittoku," mentioned above.

A *bonseki* is another fitting ornament for the

Specimens

of

Ikebana

tokonoma with the same picture. *Bonseki* is a piece of stone naturally formed in some interesting shape. Stones often have charms that appeal to the Japanese taste—in their shape, in their lines, in their hardness, and in their touch. Indeed, the study of stones would make an interesting subject for a whole book.

Ornaments made of metal, pottery, or wood, examples of industrial art, may also be placed in the *tokonoma*. These *okimono*, as the ornaments are called, may be familiar to the reader in his rounds of the art stores. For a full description of *okimono*, information must be secured from the extensive fields of sculpture and industrial art and space does not allow me to do anything like justice to this interesting topic. We at once turn to the next subject.

VI. *NANGA* SCHOOL OF PAINTING
AND AMATEUR

It may be presumed that the reader, in his travels around the country, has made a stay in a hot-spring resort in the mountains or in a small inn in a provincial town. He may have found a *tokonoma*, though a humble one, in the room to which he was shown and on the wall a *kakemono*. Over the door he may have observed a *gaku*, frame containing a picture or some writing. If the *kakemono* and *gaku* contained pictures instead of calligraphic specimens, the chances are that they are examples of the art of the *Nanga* school, so numerous are the pictures of that school.

The explanation is that *Nanga* is regarded as the art of amateurs. *Nanga* painters are found even in remote country districts. In a spa, for instance, such a visitor might make a short stay of four or five days. These amateur artists often have the habit of giving away their " masterpieces " to people with whom they come into contact. If the recipient of such a gift happens to be an innkeeper, he will have the pictures mounted for the decoration of the

Part of the "Spring Landscape" by *Taiga Ike*
(See Fig. 31)

tokonoma and the lintel, acting on the principle that anything is better than nothing. Hence the ubiquity of these amateur pictures. Now, why is *Nanga* considered especially an art for amateurs? The answer is because it is based on the ideas of the *bunjin* (men of letters) of China, who founded the art school. *Bunjin* differ somewhat from the so-called "literary men" of today. They were not only distinguished in verse and prose, but also well versed in ethics and political science. When one of them was needed by the country, he responded to the call and became an officer in the government—a minister of State or even a premier. When he was no longer needed, he returned to private life and enjoyed himself in literary pursuits. His activities were not confined to literary work; he indulged in painting to satisfy his artistic urge. The pictures he painted were not encumbered by artifice and the technical devices such as those often used by the professional artists of the art academy. Spirit not technique was what they emphasized—a spirit becoming to a free and unfettered *bunjin*.

In the Yüan and Ming dynasties in China, these literati mostly lived in the districts watered by the lower course of the Yangtze River; hence the name of *Nanga* which literally means, "South pictures," in contradistinction to the pictures by the Northern school (*Hokuga*) represented by the art academy. When the *Nanga* entered Japan in the mid-Edo period the ideas of those amateur artists were also in-

FIG. 31 "Landscape of Spring" by

troduced. It is true, the social structure of Japan
did not allow the existence of *bunjin* in the Chinese
sense, but their way of thinking seems to have struck
a responsive chord in the hearts of the cultured
Japanese. This accounts for the proud and lofty
spirit, which is embodied in the *Nanga*—an art for
amateurs possessing features that are different from
those of professional artists.

The most distinguished of the *Nanga* productions
in Japan are, in the majority of cases, the works of

Taiga Ike (Collection of Mr. I. Dan, Tōkyō)

career *Nanga* artists. The " Haku-un Kōju-Zu "
(Picture of White Clouds and Red Trees) (Pl. 8)
and the " Shunjū Sansui Byōbu " (Folding Screens
containing Landscapes of Spring and Autumn) (Fig.
31, 32) by Taiga Ike (1723-1776) and the " Shūchū
Baishōgyo Zu" (Picture of Fishermen selling Octopuses
in their Boat)(Pl. 9) by Chikuden Tanomura (1777-1835)
may be given as excellent typical examples. These
pictures exhibit the spirit of purity and freedom and
the noble sentiment of transcendentalism. In these

respect they are akin to the *sumi-e* (monochromes) of the Muromachi and Momoyama periods. Most of the paintings of the amateur *Nanga* artists are over-shadowed by the excellent work of these master artists, though exception must be made of a few—such, for instance, as the productions of Kazan Watanabe (1793-1841), a progressive statesman in the latter days of the Tokugawa regime. A similar situation existed also in China, where *Nanga* pictures of out

FIG. 32 "Landscape of Autumn" by

standing merit came, too, from the brush of the professionals.

Now, as for the essential difference between the *Nanga* and the *Hokuga*. In a word, the *Hokuga* that is, the monochromes of the Muromachi period (1392-1568), have strong, severe lines in contrast to the moderate, free, and gentle lines in *Nanga* art. This is a comparison of the extremes in both schools; there is of course a twilight zone partaking of the

Taiga Ike (Collection of Mr. I. Dan, Tōkyō)

nature of both, and the history of Japanese painting does record some instances of these hybrid productions. These pictures are exceptions. A legitimate *Nanga* may be described as a kind of monochrome, characterized by a moderation, freedom, and gentleness of lines. These lines can be made fairly well by anyone without long years of diligent practice. To the Chinese men of letters belongs the credit of discovering the fact that by the use of such lines fine pictures could be made. This easiness of approach has no doubt been a challenge to amateurs to try their hand at *Nanga*. I do not know how the matter stands at present, but, when I was a boy, third and fourth rate *Nanga* painters used to make a round of the provincial towns giving short courses in painting lasting a week or two. These art courses were attended by the art-loving youths of each locality who practised assiduously under their master's guidance with a picture-book (Fig. 33) before them and learned how to paint within the limited time at their disposal.

In *Nanga* art the first pictures painted usually have the *ran* (orchid) as models. The *ran* in pictures have slender leaves with a couple of modest looking flowers. Each of the leaf blades is drawn by a single movement of the brush. The drawing of the *ran*, therefore, furnishes the pupil with a good natural opportunity to practise line-drawing—thereby teaching him the way lines should be drawn, to perceive the psychological value of various lines, and the knack of attaining a free hand in line-drawing.

After the *ran* in progressive order comes the bamboo. In drawing the culm of a bamboo, the line representing the section between two joints is drawn vigorously in one motion, otherwise the feeling of simplified elegance is not expressed satisfactorily. The point of the blade must be rendered with a springy motion of the brush.

The next model is usually the plum-tree with its blossoms. In this stage of progress, the movements of the brush become more complicated. In a plum

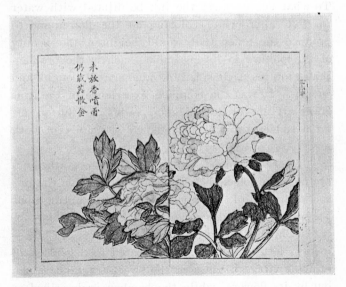

FIG. 33 A specimen of *Nanga* picture-book

picture the stem is thick and shows a rough surface, but water splashes are drawn with quick, light lines, and the twigs bearing the blossoms are made with a combination of short, strong lines. The plum finished, the chrysanthemum is taken up next. The pupil now begins to find that *Nanga* painting is not so easy as it appears at first. It is by no means an easy task to produce a resemblance to a leaf, rather complicated in shape, by a few touches of the brush. There is still another difficulty to overcome—to reproduce the flower with its dozens of petals. Shading with black ink begins to be an important problem. To what degree must the ink be diluted with water to give appropriate coloring to the flower and to produce the touch that would heighten the beauty of the picture in its ensemble—such is the problem that requires a considerable amount of thought and energy. It was the common experience of the itinerant art master at this stage in his institute to suffer a sudden drop in attendance of pupils of both sexes.

The *ran*, bamboo, blum-tree, and chrysanthemum are not only selected as subjects suitable for the initial training of beginners in *Nanga* painting, but they are chosen also for another reason. This concerns Chinese literature. In the writings of Chinese men of letters, the *ran* is compared to a gentleman of noble virtue because of the sweet fragrance given out by its flowers, while the bamboo is described as suggestive of a retainer known for his integrity.

The plum-tree, because it puts forth blossoms of pure white, is mentioned as symbolic of a man of character, and the chrysanthemum is thought of as something like a modest recluse as it seems to take pride in blooming unseen, shrouded by foliage in a hedge. These four were what the Chinese men of learning called *shikunshi*, or four gentlemen. Very likely the *Nanga* pictures that the reader has seen in the country inns and elsewhere were mostly some representation of these "four gentlemen" of the plant world.

A stone is sometimes added to a picture of one of the *shikunshi* for effect. Stones have been a favorite with the literary men of China, and from them Japanese amateur artists learned their fondness for stones. A beautiful stone certainly has qualities that appeal to the lover of beauty—a density of texture, beautiful lines, a rich response to touch. A stone that emits a metalic sound when struck, for instance, gives a feeling of repose to the beholder, when it is placed in the *tokonoma* as an ornament. A large stone of this kind makes a pleasurable object for the eye when placed between trees in a garden. The two nations place emphasis on different points in their appreciation of the esthetic qualities of decorative stones. Let me give an instance. For the Chinese, it appears that one of the qualifications necessary for an ornamental stone is that it must have a natural hole or holes, which, however, does not enter into the Japanese appreciation of stones for decorative purposes. In placing a stone in the garden, the

FIG. 34 "Snow Landscape" by Gyokudō Uragami (1745—1820)
(Collection of Mr. T. Shibata, Shiga)

FIG. 35 "Portrait of a Scholar" by Kazan Watanabe
(Collection of Mr. S. Shimomura, Kanagawa)

FIG. 36 A sketch by Kazan Watanabe (from

Chinese have a tendency to show as much of it as possible, but here in Japan, such a stone is buried deep in the ground, as if to give the impression that the visible part, like an iceberg in water, is only a small section of the bulk which is inbedded deep in the earth. This difference of treatment is reflected in the *Nanga* pictures painted by the Chinese and Japanese artists.

118 ～

the "Sights and Scenes of Four Provinces")

Besides the *shikunshi*, the plants that find most favor with the *Nanga* painters are the daffodil, lotus, peach, pear, *kaidō* (aronia), *fuyō* (*Hibiscus mutabilis*), tree-peony, and rose. As these are subjects that present considerable technical difficulty in painting, they are usually beyond the sphere of the amateur artist. There is an additional difficulty of coloring, which is essential to a certain extent in painting these plants. Landscapes are perhaps the subject that finds greatest favor with the amateurs as well as the professionals. For, like the landscapes in the monochromes of the *Hokuga* school, they afford the professionals a good means of expressing the Utopia which they dream about in their minds and, for the amateurs, they provide a convenient elasticity that allows even those of meager attainments to produce something that is like a picture.

The word more about *Nanga* paintings. The artists love to couple them with a poem, which is sometimes written by the same person and sometimes by another. Such a poem should be in perfect accord as to nature and tone with the picture to which it is wedded. This has given birth to the theory originating in Japan and China that poetry and picture are one. With the Greeks of old, the Orientals have thought that poetry is painting with a voice and painting is poetry without voice. In the Far East, there is another similar theory—that of the identity of calligraphy and painting. This does not mean that the handwriting of the poem written as an adjunct to a *Nanga* picture must be in congenial with it, though this is of course to be desired if possible. What is meant is that both calligraphy and painting concern themselves with lines representative of the character and dignity of the man who practises them. This is regarded by the Orientals as one of the basic principles of art.

FIG. 37 "Thoreauesque Life in the Mountains"
from the "Jūben Jūgi"
A typical *Nanga* sketch by Buson Yosa,
famous poet-painter of the Edo period.

VII. BEAUTIES IN COLOR PRINTS

It is likely that most of the foreign visitors in this country have seen something of Japanese color prints (*ukiyo-e*), as excellent examples of this type of art are found in museums and private collections in Europe and America. Perhaps the Boston Museum of Fine Arts has the richest collections of these prints in the world. There are excellent collections in Europe though inferior both in quantity and quality to that in Boston, in Paris, London, and elsewhere. It is probable that there are many people in the West who think that Japanese painting is represented only by the color print.

As a matter of fact, however, the color print is by no means the only painting of Japan, as what has already been said in these pages attest. It is no more than a branch—a special branch—of Japanese painting. The monochromes, which belong to the *Hokuga*, the *Nanga*, and the *Yamato* and decorative pictures, which are creation by Japanese artists— these are the legitimate branches of Japanese painting. Their characteristics, to put it briefly, are

"A Courtesan" Hand-painted by *Chōshun Miyagawa*
(Collection of Mr. C. Shibusawa,
Yokohama)

Oriental idealism and ornamentation, purely esthetic. In all of these, the object aimed at is the production of dignified elegance. Hence it is that these legitimate pictures are considered worthy of being hung in the *tokonoma*, which is the place of honor and artistic taste in the Japanese home. Perhaps this is their chief use. Such is not the case with the color print, which is rarely mounted and hung in the *tokonoma*.

Color prints are never idealistic, nor are they decorative in object. *Ukiyo-e*, which is the Japanese term for the color print, means a picture illustrative of the life of the common people. Naturally such pictures are intended first to appeal to the sentiment and perception of contemporary people. Their subjects are also a little too plebeian, too often found dishabille to be in keeping with the dignity of the *tokonoma*. The prints are that type of art which should be laid away in the dress cabinet of the mistress or on a shelf and taken out occasionally for the pleasure of the eye. It is true that there is a sort of dignified elegance in a color print, but this is the case in all objects of art, pictures included. Though that dignified elegance based on *kihin* (moral value) to the Japanese might be seen with different eyes by the people of the West.

Ukiyo-e in their earliest days were chiefly painted by hand, not printed. (Fig. 38) In these early specimens, the figure of a courtesan, for instance, is painted with strong lines true to tradition. These

FIG. 38 "Courtesan" Hand-painting by Dohan (in the beginning of the 18th cent.)

pictures began to be reproduced in print in the mid-Edo period (18th cent.), and it was only in the latter years of the Tokugawa regime that they were called *nishiki-e*, or multi-colored *bro ade* pictures. They were made by using some dozen blocks for printing in as many different colors. The wood-block print represents the work of three co-operators —the painter, the engraver, and the pressman—and so painstaking and conscientious were the print-makers that an edition was limited to 30 or 40 copies, or 70 or 80 at the most.

The majority of the color prints depict actors and beauties. Pictures of actors were favorites of the people, because the citizens of Edo (now Tōkyō) in those days were fanatic lovers of the *kabuki* plays. And this popularity of actors' pictures may be compared to the huge sales which photographs of screen players command in these days. People in the Edo period, specially womenfolk, never failed to go to the theaters when successful play was running. And they were very careful to purchase color prints of the actors who were drawing big houses. It was not necessary that these pictures be good likenesses of the players presenting their expressions realistically. It was sufficient in most cases if the make-up of the actors was shown satisfactorily. Whom the portraits represented, was readily known by the family crests their costumes bore. Regular play-goers though the Edo people were, they valued the sight of those portraits which brought to their imagination vividly the

FIG. 39 Kabuki Actor　by Sharaku　(National Museum of Tōkyō)

FIG. 40 Kabuki Actors by Sharaku (National Museum of Tōkyō)

features of the actors in character, the setting, and the development of the plots. Let us take the case of Sharaku (18th cent.). (Fig. 39, 40) He made many actor pictures, but he did not think it necessary to give his portraits individuality. The actors he painted have eyes that are invariably small, oval, and slanting. The noses and lips are of two or three types. The portraits cannot be said to be true to the originals, but one feels that the actors represented wore expressions that were appropriate to the characters they impersonated and the language they used. One has to conclude that, in Sharaku's case, it was his aim to impart a sort of dignity to his pictures by conventionalization which is traditional in Japanese painting.

The same thing may be said of the pictures of the beauties. It will be observed that the fair women portrayed by Harunobu (1725—1770), who is known as the pioneer of the multi-colored prints (*nishiki-e*), are of a uniform type—with faces as innocent as a child's, skin soft and delicate, eyes devoid of distinct expression. What is more characteristic is that they have abnormally small hands and feet—so diminutive almost that they might belong to people in ill health. This is the case with daughters of the *samurai* as with women of the town. In extreme cases, as, for instance, in " Setchū Aiaigasa " (Man and Woman under an Umbrella) (Fig. 41), even the man is pictured thus, so that in Harunobu's works the difference between the sexes can

128 ～

鈴木春信画

FIG. 41 "Man and Woman under an Umbrella"

by Harunobu Suzuki

FIG. 42 "Beauty visiting a Shrine on a Rainy Night"

by Harunobu Suzuki

FIG. 43 "Around the Clock with Young Girls"
by Utamaro Kitagawa

FIG. 44 One of the " Ten Women with Different Physiognomies "
by Utamaro Kitagawa

be distinguished only through the costume and coiffeur.

How is this peculiarity of Harunobu's prints to be explained? The remarks made of the actor pictures do not apply here. It is known that he used two models for his pictures of women. One was named Osen, an attractive girl working in a tea-house in the enclosure of the Kasamori Inari Shrine in Yanaka, Edo—a tea-house which had a number of benches placed on the grounds for the accommodation of the customers. Here Osen served them tea and cake. The other model was Ofuji, the daughter of a tooth-pick maker in Asakusa. Even admitting that the two girls were exceptionally beautiful, one cannot suppose that Harunobu merely hoped to portray them so as to arouse pleasurable excitement in the bosoms of the people of Edo by reminding them of their fair originals whose charms were the talk of the town. It is more likely that the objective Harunobu had in mind was something else. He wanted to represent in his pictures the frailty, beauty and coquettishness, not of any particular woman, but of the gentle sex in general which was regarded as a sort of doll in those days. This may be gathered from the poses which his women take. They never stand erect like a pole. Some have their heads inclined forward, some are turning back, others are bowing low. They step out in postures that are full of pretty curves. Their flowing costumes help to enhance their feminine charms when they assume

FIG. 45 "Beauty at a Tea-house" by Kiyonaga Torii

FIG. 46　"Woman dressing her Hair"　by Kunisada Utagawa

those poses. In such postures, the collar of the *kimono*, usually gathered neatly in front, becomes loosened and the sleeves fall back exposing the arms. The folded skirts, too, are forced slightly open by the movement of the legs. For a picture typical of Harunobu's beauties I refer the reader to "Yoru-no-Ame Miyamairi Bijin Zu" (Picture of a Beauty Visiting a Shrine on a Rainy Night). (Fig. 42)

The erotic suggestiveness of such a picture is further accentuated by the tenderness of the lines. Even the outlines and the creases of the *kimono* take on a fascination sensual in feeling. Color again contribute to the effect, as in pictures of the West. The multi-colored print is glorified most in Harunobu's pictures. It is the opinion of some critics that Harunobu painted his beauties with hands and legs conspicuously small-sized, because he designed to bring out in them a prettiness that is sensuous, decadent, and, in a sense, morbid.

Just as Harunobu's beauties are of a fixed type, so Utamaro (1754-1806) gave his beauties a feature common to all of them. That feature is the air of sophistication which they all possess. Even in the picture "Musume Hidokei" (Around the Clock with Young Girls) (Fig. 43), in which the title indicates that young girls are intended, the "girl" is really a mature woman. Utamaro's women are invariably long-faced and they have eyes so narrow that they look like bits of string, yet how coquettish they are in their dreamy suggestion! One might

PLATE X   Shaka Nyorai by *Tori*
                (Bronze: Hōryūji Temple, Nara)

PLATE XI

Shaka Nyorai
(Bronze: Jinda
Temple, Tōkyō

PLATE XII Kichijōten (Wood: Jōruriji Temple, Kyōto pref.)

expect that of the women of pleasure at Yoshiwara, but even girls in the business quarters attired in *kimono* with black collars are similarly represented. All his women are, without exception, tall and slender, a characteristic he emphasizes by a long skirt drawn behind.

Utamaro also had models for his pictures of beauties, the best known being Okita, the popular waitress of a tea-house in Asakusa. The beauties of Harunobu and Utamaro differed according to the features of their models, but they had some points of similarity. The two artists painted their beauties in postures that exhibited sex appeal and in costumes that were arranged so their lines strengthen that appeal. This is especially noticeable in the picture of the beauty combing her hair, one of the series of " Fujin Sōgaku Jittai " (Ten Women with Different Physiognomies). (Fig. 44) Such postures and semi-nudity as are seen in this series are common in Western paintings, but fairly rare in Japanese. In these pictures the lines of the body are slender and smooth, suggesting the feeling that the flesh utterly lacks elasticity. It seems that soft-fleshed skin like this was considered a things of beauty in those olden days. Like Harunobu, Utamaro painted his men, whether they were young men in *okosozukin* (a headgear originated from that of a high priest) or a burgher's son on his way to the pleasure quarter of Yoshiwara, to match his beauties, making them show not masculine strength, but a tenderness and gentleness more suitable to the fair sex.

After all, this may be interpreted as a reflection of the decadent social conditions prevailing in the latter days of the Edo period. This lack of chastity in the women and the effeminacy of the male is not confined to the productions of Harunobu and Utamaro; it can also be observed in the pictures of other color-print artists, such as Kiyonaga (1752-1815) and Toyoharu (1735-1814). The beauties painted by Kiyonaga, for instance, in "Ryōgoku Shūyū Zu" (Picture of a Boat Picnic at Ryōgoku), have a dignified bearing suggestive of their gentle birth and upbringing. (Fig. 45) Similarly the beauties of Toyoharu, in "Suirō Yūen Zu" (Picture of a Banquet at a River-side Restaurant), possess the glamour of sinister fascination. In all these cases, the artists aimed at presenting an appeal to decadent and sensuous love.

In these respect, the beauties of Kunisada (1786-1864) are no exceptions to the general rule, though, in his case, the taste of the artist is somewhat different from the other artists. He, like his brothers of the brush, drew his beauties according to type but they are represented, not as passive objects solely for pleasure, but as women with a certain pride. On occasions, they look even strong-willed and manly. Their flesh, too, is not of that soft, unelastic, and unhealthy color seen in the work of other beauty artists of the period, but his heroines are more robust-looking, as for instance the woman looking at her coiffeur with a pair of looking glasses, one of the "Fujo Hakkei" (Eight views of Woman). (Fig. 46) In this picture, the woman is painted with her muscles fairly well developed, her flesh elastic, her chest normal. There is realism; here, one feels that the blood of life is circulating through her.

After Kunisada no color-print artist worthy of mention has appeared. The Revolution of Meiji, which took place soon after, marked an epoch in Japan's history. Things underwent a complete metamorphosis, and the *ukiyo-e* receded suddenly to the background.

VIII. THE WORLD OF BUDDHA

(Part I.)

The reader may have had occasion, on trips to various places in Japan, to see something of Japanese sculpture as well as Japanese painting. He may have been somewhat surprised to find that most examples of Japanese sculpture are associated with Buddhism. A full appreciation of Japanese sculpture, therefore, is made difficult for people of the West as the figures cast in bronze or worked in wood, were subjected to various restrictions required by the Buddhist faith. It is true that many pieces of European sculpture can only be appreciated with a knowledge of classic mythology and Christianity, but this class of sculpture is diminishing in number, and there is a growing number of masterpieces in the modern style that is free from classical associations. But this is not the case with Japanese sculpture. In the Momoyama and Edo periods (1568-1867), which may appropriately be described as modern, sculpture was declining in popularity, scarcely any specimens worthy of mention being produced in these periods. Sculpture antidating this time were almost all associated with Buddhism.

It is a difficult task to give justice to the wide subject of Buddhism in this brief sketch—so rich and ramified are its teachings and principles. A comprehensive description would be out of place here, so only that part of the Buddhist lore that concerns sculpture will be treated in the following pages. Buddhism as manifested in sculpture was first represented by a group of Nyorai. Nyorai (*Tathagata*) means a concrete manifestation of the absolute truth of the universe as conceived by Buddhists ; it is practically equivalent to Buddha. Buddha, who was born on this planet and became a historic character, is known as " Shaka." The truth of the universe as embodied by Shaka has many phases or attributes. These phases are variously represented by Nyorai prefixed by descriptive terms—Shaka Nyorai, Yakushi Nyorai, Amida Nyorai, and so forth.

The most famous image of Shaka Nyorai is the one in bronze in the possession of the Hōryūji Temple in a suburb of Nara. (Pl. 10) It belongs to the early stage of the Nara period (645-794). The figure together with two attendants, each standing on the god's right and left, is the work of Tori, a descendant of a Chinese naturalized in Japan. This alien blood in the sculptor accounts for the peculiarities in features and stature, which are somehow continental in impression, and which distinguish the image from the native pieces of sculpture produced in later generations. The head is not in proportion to the size of the body. This unrealism is explained thus by some critics : These differences come from the customs of faith and worship as they prevailed in those olden days. People sat on their knees and, looking up with their backs still bent down, it seemed that the big head impressed them with a deeper sense of reverence, as if in expectation of some special grace to be granted. This interpretation is universally endorsed by specialists. In the icon in question the hands, too, are disproportionately large. The right hand, opened, is lifted breast-high, and the left hand, also opened, is placed, with the palm up, on his lap, showing that Shaka is preaching. This arrangement of hands serves as an identification of Shaka so that he will not be mistaken for other deity. It was this point that Tori wanted to emphasize when he exaggerated the size of the hands. A parallel is observed in European art. In the "Venus de Milo," one of the world's masterpieces in art, differing from the Hōryūji Shaka Nyorai, the head is too small for the body. This apparent defect, however, is really a merit as the physical beauty of the goddess is thereby enhanced and the face crowning the body is conspicuous in stability and has dignity added to beauty.

Tori's Shaka Nyorai is outstanding for its compelling strength, and for this it is entitled to be ranked as a masterpiece. Strength is not invariably an attribute of Buddhist sculpture ; there are some that are gentle-featured and appeal to the esthetic

Kichijōten   (Painted on wood ; see Pl. 12)

sense. As an instance of this I mention the one owned by the Jindaiji, a temple in the suburbs of Tōkyō. (Pl. 11) Presumably this figure dates from the latter part of the Nara period. It represents Shaka Nyorai smiling, and it somehow puts the beholder in a social mood. It is realistic in effect, the proportion of the body and the head being almost natural. There is another fine figure of Shaka Nyorai at the Murōji Temple in Nara prefecture, though this was produced at a somewhat later date, during the early years of the Heian period (794-1185). (Pl. 11)

It appears that one of the Nyorai was popularly believed to be a healer of ills. In this remote age, when the art of healing had not advanced to its present efficiency, it is likely that the people believed the restoration of health was a function which religious faith alone could perform. This Nyorai physician is Yakushi Nyorai, whose name literally means healer. This Buddhist benefactor is usually represented as carrying a small medicine pot in his left hand, which symbolizes that the bearer is a doctor. The most celebrated of the statues of Yakushi Nyorai is the one in the possession of the Yakushiji Temple in the suburbs of Nara. (Fig. 47) The figure which stands on a pedestal of marble has stability and a look of supreme majesty. Japanese Buddhists perceive in that stability a hope for eternity. This gilded bronze statue was casted in the early days of the Nara period, and, because of its later age, it shows a more refined art than the Shaka Nyorai from the chisel of such an early master as Tori. The proportion of the parts of the body is admirable and the folds of the garments are entirely natural. A study of the skilful workmanship gives one a pleasurable feeling of admiration. Especially noteworthy is the facial expression of the Nyorai. Dignity there certainly is, but not to such an extent as to forbid a familiar approach—the strength is happily tempered with softness. The golden medium is suggestive of a perfect harmony of human virtues, worthy of a Nyorai, which is a personification of truth. Possessing such a merit, the statue is well entitled to the praise that it is one of the finest examples of Japanese sculpture, representing the highest watermark of the art. It is not surprising that no other image of Yakushi Nyorai can match this specimen in merit. For the information of the reader, it may be noted here that there is a beautiful feminine figure of Buddhist origin, which, like the image of Yakushi Nyorai, is carrying a round object in its left hand. This is the figure of Kisshō-ten, a female deity whose duty was the dispensation of human happiness. The round object is not a medicine pot, but an emblem of wealth, a jewel invested with power to bring good luck to man. One of these figures is the property of the Jōruriji Temple, the date attributed to it being the middle of the Heian period. (Pl. 12) It is carved in wood and plastered in color. It has a very pretty look, and is a fine example of feminine beauty in the Heian age.

FIG.47 Yakushi Nyorai (Bronze: Yakushiji Temple, Nara)

Included in the group of Nyorai is Amida, or
Mida (*Amitabha*). *Amitabha* is Sanscrit meaning
"light," and it is symbolic of the essence of truth
which administers salvation to humanity without restraint. One distinguishing feature of Amida is that
he holds his hands on his lap and his fingers and
thumbs appear as circles. A considerable number of

⌒ 145

statues of this Nyorai, the oldest one dating from the Nara period, have been handed down to us, and the one which is said to be the greatest of them all is that in the Hōōdō (Phoenix Hall) at Uji. (Fig. 48) This is the work of Jōchō (?—1057), a famous sculptor of the Heian period. The Hōōdō itself is an example of architecture that is outstanding in elegance and beauty. I like to think of it as a piece of frozen music of marvelous excellence. The workmanship of the Amida Nyorai, however, makes it well worthy as being enshrined in that structure. The figure has a fine countenance, exhibiting such a warmth of heart and magnanimity of spirit that the worshipper cannot help but believe that the Nyorai has power to pardon the blackest of sins and lead him on to Paradise. The body and posture of the image leave nothing to be desired. In the figure one sees serenity, elegance and symmetry almost unequalled in Buddhist sculpture anywhere. Needless to say, such a work of art is highly appreciated by believers of the faith. As an artistic production it has a wealth of characteristics peculiar to the Japanese.

In the pantheon of Buddhist gods, Buddha or Nyorai is of course the main figure, occupying a central position, but there are other gods that inspire a far wider devotion. These gods are Kannon (*Avalokitesvara*). A Kannon is a goddess, and a dispenser of motherly benevolence. She is sometimes paired with Amida as an attendant, but, in most,

FIG. 48   Amida Nyorai
(Bronze:　Hōōdō, Byōdōin, Kyōto)

FIG. 49 Sake-kai Kannon (Wood: Hōryūji Temple, Nara)

FIG. 50 Yumedono Kannon (Wood:
Hōryūji Temple, Nara)

FIG. 52 Part of the Nyoirin Kannon (Fig. 51)

(opposite page)

FIG. 51 Nyoirin Kannon (Wood: Chūgūji Temple, Nara)

cases, she stands alone, and it is believed that she listens to the confessions of the guilty in spirit and answers their prayers. In a sense, she may be said to occupy the position in Buddhism that the Virgin Mary does in Roman Catholicism. Seekers after grace naturally turn with more confidential hope to a woman than a man and therefore tender-hearted Kannon than the sterner Nyorai is worshipped more commonly. This worship of Kannon has had a long history in Japan. Statues of the goddess were sculptured in abundance as early as the Nara period, and many of these productions are of excellent workmanship. The Hōryūji Temple has three of these masterpieces. One is a wooden statue placed in the Kondō and popularly called Sake-kai Kannon (*Saké*-purchasing Kannon)—a name give to her because she has something like a *saké* bottle hanging from her left hand. (Fig. 49) The reason why she is going to buy *saké* is not known, but the image is beautiful beyond the power of language to express. Her face is quiet and placid. Her lips adorned with a faint smile overflow with the spirit of benevolence. The lines that stream from neck to the shoulders, to the breast and the legs are perfectly realistic and yet are pregnant with artistic dignity and beauty. Another famous statue is Yumedono Kannon, which was concealed in the Yumedono of the Hōryūji Temple away from public view for ten long centuries. (Fig. 50) This Kannon also carved of wood and is in a standing posture. It has a handsome countenance, intellectual and calm. When the light falls on it from a certain angle, it has a weird look, the last thing to be expected in an impersonation of benevolence. The image was wrapped in cloth during its years of hiding up to the early years of the Meiji era (1868-1912), and this has given it an unnatural appearance of age, which is responsible for its highly mystic lure.

The third and perhaps best of this famous trio is Nyoirin Kannon owned by the Chūgūji Temple, which is separated from the Hōryūji by an intervening garden. (Fig. 51, 52) This Kannon is also carved in wood (camphor-tree), but is not a statue. The goddess is sitting on a bench, with her left leg resting on her right knee. Her cheek is lightly supported by her hand and her elbow rests on the right knee. There are indications that this image was elaborately painted in colors and gilded when it was made, but the coating has worn off and the grain of the wood can be seen. The surface has darkened into a purplish brown from the smoke of centuries of burning incense and it gives off a faint luster. The breast and the chest show realistic and esthetic curve. This figure ranks high among the famous pieces of sculpture in the world. The countenance is well proportioned. The eyes are half closed in contemplation suggesting a tenderness of heart and the smile lingering on the lips is affectionate and warm-hearted, unlike the expression of the Kannon in the Yumedono. The trio which it is the good fortune of the Hōryūji to possess certainly have high merits viewed not as objects of worship, but simply as works of art with contemporary women as models. In this they differ from the Nyorai in which splendor and beauty are too highly idealized. In the three images there are subtleties of expression which are individualistic in effect. In the Kōryūji Temple near Kyōto there is a Nyoirin Kannon, which, though it does not come up to the level of the trio in artistic merit, is celebrated for the success of the sculptor in embodying feminine beauty.

Next to the Kannon should be mentioned the figures of Jizō Bosatsu. A Bosatsu is an attendant or an assistant of a Nyorai. A Kannon should properly be described as one of the Bosatsu. Jizō Bosatsu is a guardain god for children. Hence the kindly expression of his face, though he is of the masculine sex. His head is clean shaven, perhaps because it is believed that the exposure of the shape of the head, which is harmonious in development, best emphasizes a gracious magnanimity of heart. A typical specimen may be seen in the one in the Tōdaiji Temple at Nara, the work of Kaikei. (Fig. 53) Kaikei was an artist who flourished in the Kamakura period (1185-1394), which seems to have been the time when a belief in Jizō Bosatsu was in great vogue. The Jizō in question is well fleshed, gentle in demeanor and innocent in expression, as is becoming to a guardian of the young.

There is another statue made by Kaikei which

FIG. 53 Jizō Bosatsu by Kaikei (Wood: Tōdaiji Templ₂, Nara)

FIG. 54 One of the Shitennō (Wood: Kaidan-in, Tōdaiji Temple, Nara)

is also in the Tōdaiji. It is named "Sōgyō Hachiman," and represents a priest in a sitting position. Hachiman is one of the Japanese gods, and, in this particular instance, he is shown as a convert to the Buddhist faith as may be gathered from his shaven head and Buddhist attire. This figure has a gentle and childish-looking face. We Japanese have a fondness for such a type of face.

There are many other types of Buddhist sculpture differing from those already mentioned. Some of these are soldiers and strong men guarding truth against the destructive violence of the devils and the heathens. Specially noteworthy are the "Shitennō Zō" (four guardians) (Fig. 54) installed in the Kaidan-in at the Tōdaiji Temple, the pair of Kongō Rikishi (adamant guardians) or Niō (two guardians of the gate) at the Nandai-mon, south entrance to the same temple. (Fig. 24, 25) The former belong to the Nara period while the latter are the works of the master sculptors Unkei and Kaikei in the Kamakura period. The Nara warriors are armored and armed, with countenances strained in anger. The Niō are scantily attired, their loins wrapped with a piece of drapery. Accordingly the masculine development of their frames and the sinews and swelling of their flesh are distinctly visible. It may be presumed that the sculptors hoped to express roughness and ferociousness in the features and also to give a vivid realistic effect. These figures are well deserving of a place among the best of this class of sculpture in this country. In most cases, the Niō are installed, one on either side of the main gate in a large temple and are meant to function as its guards. It sometimes happens that a pair of lions take the place of the Niō, though they are usually found in Shinto shrines. The king of beasts as used in Japanese sculpture is conventionalized *a la chinoise*, but it differs in style from the dogs placed at the gates of temples or palaces in China. No description will be made here of the *kara-jishi* as the lion is called in Japanese, on the supposition that the reader may have had occasion to witness some specimens of these shrine ornaments. The Chinese dog is evidently connected with Shamanism, and when we consider the fact that it is kindred to the Sphinx of Egypt, we are led to imagine that Japanese sculpture may be remotely linked with Egyptian culture though the connection is yet obscure. Speaking of foreign influences in Japanese art, one recalls that in Japanese sculpture, especially in the Nyorai, the Indian influence is fairly evident. Their wavy hair is clearly traceable to the Gandara art and the *rahatsu* (small clusters of curls like the seeds of the malonier) on their heads are a characteristic in common use in the art of that school.

Japanese sculpture no doubt has examples, such as statues, for instance, which do not belong to the world of Buddha. Some of these may possess artistic excellence, but of these no words of explanation are necessary, as they are easily understood and appreciated by the reader without the aid of any accompanying information.

IX. THE WORLD OF BUDDHA

(Part 2)

The world of Buddha has had representation in Japanese art not only in sculpture but also, naturally, in painting. Western travelers who have visited Kyōto and Nara must have seen some of these Buddhist paintings. Some of the more observant may have noticed that Buddhism in Japanese paintings has features a little different from those in sculpture. The same Buddhist world is viewed from different angles by the painter and the sculptor, and the result is that there is a difference in the choice of their Buddhistic themes. To be precise, while in sculpture the representation take the form of a quantitative expression of the countenance and the posture of the individual Buddha and Bosatsu, in painting most of the pictures are made the means of illustrating the ideas of Buddhistic philosophy and tales from Buddhistic literature.

These illustrative pictures with a Buddhist motif were produced in as remote an age as the beginning of the Nara period (645-794). An example is the *mitsuda-e* painted on the side and doors of the

FIG. 55 Tamamushi-no-Zushi (a miniature shrine),
Hōryūji Temple, Nara

celebrated miniature shrine called "Tamamushi-no-Zushi." (Fig. 55) A *mitsuda-e* is a kind of oil painting in which the colors are mixed with a drying agent—lead oxide—and dissolved in *enoabura*, a vegetable oil. The country from which this method of painting originated seems to be Persia, where it was discovered in the 4th or 5th century of the Christian era. The art somehow found its way to Japan, presumably through India and China. *Mitsuda* pictures, however, have showed no further development, the field having been dominated here by brush and ink painting. In the West, thanks to the valuable contributions of Van Eyck brothers in the 13th century to the art of oil painting, this method has achieved the marked progress as it shows today. On the other hand, in Japan the *mitsuda-e* has been greatly neglected, its use being limited mainly to the decoration of lacquer ware.

It may be remarked in passing that there are evidences that the art flourished in the Nara period showing distinct Persian influence. In the Shōsō-in, an Imperial treasury of antiques which are in an almost perfect state of preservation, among the household articles, such as table ware, textile fabrics, and toilet articles used by the sovereigns in the Nara dynasty, there are a few specimens of this art with shapes and designs that are plainly Persian.

The Tamamushi-no-Zushi, of which a description follows, may be said to have these characteristics. This household shrine is decorated with the gorgeous wings of the *tamamushi* (*chrysochroa elegans*) pasted on in various designs and lacquered over. Another thing deserving special mention is the metal fittings in which the motif of the design is the *nindo* or honey-suckle. (Fig. 56) This plant is to be found only on the eastern shores of the Mediterranean, and used very frequently in the arts of Persia, Egypt, and Greece.

And now for a few words on the character of the Buddhist pictures on the Tamamushi shrine. On the doors in front there are paintings of two deities, Brahma and Indra, who are regarded in Indian philosophy, which is mythological in nature, as the creator and ruler of the universe. On the doors at the right and the left four Bosatsu are pictured. These, of course, cannot be said to be descriptive pictures—being the representation in painting of what another artist would have expressed in sculpture.

The picture on the back of the shrine, however, which is a painting of a *tahō-tō* (a multi-storied pagoda) is more of a descriptive nature. In the center of the picture is the pagoda, a two-storied one, the upper story being circular and the lower one square, with a five-ringed pagoda on both sides. Over the main pagoda hang the sun and the moon. An angel with her garments flowing in the air is shown in flight, and sacred birds float among the clouds with their wings spread. The figure of an Arakan making his spiritual devotions is visible in the cave of a mountain. An Arakan or Rakan is a person who devotes himself wholly to the task of attaining salvation, and who has not yet reached the status of a Bosatsu. It is not certain to which passage in the Buddhist sutras, the picture has reference but it certainly depicts a scene which is illusory and mystifying.

The *shumiza*, the stand on which a box-shaped palace containing an image of Buddha is placed, contains a picture presumably illustrative of a passage from "Jartaka," an account of the pre-mundane careers of Shaka for scores of generation. On the left side of the throne there is depicted a scene entitled "Shashin Shiko" (Feeding a Tigress by sacrificing One's Self.) (Fig. 56) It refers to a time in one of Shaka's pre-existences when he was a prince in a small kingdom of India. One day he met a hungry tigress in a bamboo grove. The tigress had a litter of seven cubs, and for want of food she was on the verge of starvation. Moved by this pathetic sight, the prince made up his mind to sacrifice his person for the benefit of the starving animal. This heroic resolve was carried out. The upper part of the picture represents the prince taking off his clothes and hanging them on a tree. In the middle section, he is shown throwing himself to the beast head foremost, and the bottom picture shows the scene where he is being greedily devoured by the beast. The three scenes shown in the three sections of the picture are consecutive in time. This is an early specimen of the narrative form adopted in painting.

FIG. 56 "Shashin Shiko" (the picture on the left side of the stand of the Tamamushi-no-Zushi)

The picture on the front of the stand shows the bones of the hero prince who gave his life to the starving tigress being consecrated by two Brahmins burning incense. The officiating priests are guarded by sacred animals which are depicted in an attitude of restraint, and in the air above angels are on the wing. The prince is received by these angels who carry him away beyond the clouds until he makes rebirth as Shaka. The story is indeed primitive and yet it is attractive in its naturalness. The brilliancy and urbanity with which the characters are portrayed are in perfect keeping with this beautiful imaginative piece. This decorative treatment of a subject is traceable to the objects found in the excavations at Lo-lang, Korea, and in the earlier productions of the Six-dynasty period (386-588) in China. It can thus be inferred that Japanese painting in the Nara period was under the influence of those ancient efforts in artistic activity in foreign lands.

Buddhist pictures in the Nara period were influenced not only by the gorgeous technique of the Six-dynasty period in China, but also by the realism and splendor of style of the Ajanta art of India. The best examples of this latter art are the twelve famous fresco painting in the Kondō or Main Hall of the Hōryūji Temple. These are painted on wall spaces of varying sizes in the hall. The pictures afford glimpses into the world of Buddha known as " Shihō-jōdo." The masterpieces are a pictorial rendering

Kannon-Bosatsu, one of the attendants of Amida Nyorai
(part of the fresco shown on the next page)

PLATE XIII

A part of the wall-painting on the west wall of the Hōryūji Temple
showing Amida Nyorai with two attendants, Kannon-Bosatsu on his
left and Seiji Bosatsu on his right. The fresco was painted more
than one thousand years ago.

of the philosophy held by a group of early Buddhists. The *Shihō-jōdo* is the world of truth symbolically represented by four Buddhas—Amida, Hōshō, Yakushi, and Shaka, and is perceived by humankind as a sacred land, a paradise, a land of happiness and plenty. These Buddhas are painted, on the major walls of the Kondō, while on the minor walls appear a number of Bosatsu, Kannon, Seiji (*Mahasthamaprapta*), Fugen (*Samantabhadra*) and others.

The frescos are painted on walls of mortar six inches thick, and consist of outlines drawn with a brush and covered with pigments which are of a mineral origin. The execution is marvellous, viewed from the technique of painting. They are dessins done by a hand full of confidence and trained to the highest level. There is a pleasing naturalness in the features and poses of Buddha and the Bosatsu. The proportions of the bodily parts are exactly correct. The bone structure and the sinews indicate that the painter was a master having at his finger-tips almost all the anatomical knowledge available on the subject. The outlines are of great beauty, especially in the arms of the Kannon which are stretched out slightly. These lines are drawn with a beautiful effect that cannot be excelled. It can be said that recognition and appreciation of esthetic quality of the "line," upon which Japanese painting is based, first drawned in those wall pictures. Naturally one wonders who could have been the author of such distinguished works of art. From ancient times up to the present, there have been various statements and conjectures regarding the artist who painted them, but none are conclusive. The most correct answer, therefore, is that the author is unknown. All that we can say is that the paintings have many points of resemblance to the Indian frescos of Ajanta and to some of the wall paintings of Western Chinese Tartary which belong to the same school of painting as the Ajanta pictures. The countenances of Buddha and the Bosatsu, for instance, are Indian, suggesting that their originals were of an alien. One may point to the noses which are Grecian in type, the long, horizontal eyes tapering off narrowly and the crescent shaped eyebrows reminding the observer that these are features entirely absent in the work of the Chinese and Koreans. There is a decidedly Indian touch in the delineation of the body, which is fleshy and somewhat sensuous. If speculation is allowed to have full play, we may venture to say that this style of painting, which originated in India, found its way into China in the Six-dynasty period through Western Chinese Tartary, and came to Japan, in a form not yet fully Sinicized. The Hōryūji frescos may belong to this group. And as a matter of fact, there is evidence pointing to this surmise. It is a fact that some of the Buddhist stone images found at Tatung and Yunkang, productions of a people plainly alien in race to the Chinese, bear close resemblance to the frescos in the Hōryūji Temple.

There is a class of paintings which may be regarded as a graphic exposition of philosophic thought in Buddhism. This type of art is known as *mandara*. *Mandara* originally meant a platform made of earth piled up. On the dais there are flowers and incense arranged in the positions specified by the doctrines. This is intended as a seat of honor for Buddha and the Bosatsu. Using this platform as an altar, the worshipper offers mystic prayers. This has been the customary practice followed from early times by believers of the Shingon sect of Buddhism. A *mandara* is a picture in which Buddha and the Bosatsu, who are waiting to be invited to occupy the dais, stand in various sections of the canvas. In other words it is a fanciful pictorial representation of the seating arrangement of the saints fixed by the doctrines concerning the functions and status of Buddha and the Bosatsu.

Being a sort of diagram, it is simple and uninteresting as a picture. The Shingon sect was a branch of Buddhism which had influence in the days of the Heian dynasty which succeeded the Nara period; consequently a considerable number of *mandara* have been handed down to us, and it is likely that the reader may have occasion to see some in old temples. A *mandara* is usually executed in this fashion; the canvas is sectioned off into spaces which may be square or round, and in these spaces Buddha or the Bosatsu are placed. In a more elaborate *mandara*, the splendor of a Buddhist paradise, for instance, is pictured. "Tenju-koku Mandara," owned by the Chū-

gūji Temple, is an example of this type. (Fig. 57)
It is on a piece of embroidered wall drapery, and because of this it may not be classed as a picture in
the strict sense of the world. It was fashioned sometime in the Nara period, and, being the work of
some Chinese craftsmen naturalized in Japan, its
characters and flowers are all conventionalized in
the Six-dynasty style. Coming down to the Heian
period, we find, for instance, " Kasuga Mandara "
and " Fudō Mandara." These are picture of Kasuga
Myōjin and Fudō Myōō and each has a small diagram
of the doctrines connected with the *mandara*. These
represent deviations from the original rules regarding the *mandara*.

In the large collection of pictures connected with
Buddhism there is another group called " Raigō Zu,"
which are pictorial illustrations of the doctrines and
creed of the Jōdo sect. This sect emphasizes the infinite love of Amida Nyorai which entitles anyone,
without exception, to work out his salvation by the
mere invocation of his holy name. *Raigō* means a
soul being led to paradise by Nyorai himself. The
Jōdo sect was founded at about the end of the Heian
period (794—1185), and attained the height of its
prosperity in the Kamakura period (1185—1394).
Naturally the " Raigō Zu " were painted most pro-
lifically in the days when the sect enjoyed its greatest vogue.

The most outstanding picture of this class is the
" Nijūgo Bosatsu Raigō Zu " painted by priest Eshin.

(Fig. 58) In this masterpiece the main deity, Amida Nyorai, is in the center, with Kannon and Seiji at his left and right. A number of Bosatsu borne on clouds come slowly down to earth while harps are played, drums beaten and sacred songs of paradise are sung. The bit of earth visible far below shows

FIG. 57 "Tenjukoku Mandara" (Scenes of Paradise), Chūgūji Temple, Nara

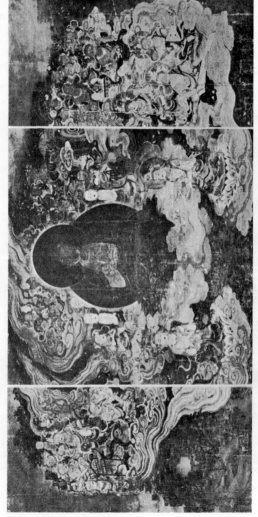

FIG. 58 "Nijūgo (廿五) Bosatsu Raigō Zu" (Daien-in Monastery, Mt. Kōya, Wakayama pref.)

FIG. 59 "Yamagoe Amida" (Amida emerging from behind the Mountains), Kinkai-Kōmyōji Temple, Kyōto

mountains, ponds, trees, and a human habitation. In the house there is a religious person, about to breathe his last, but resting assured that, because he has called upon the sacred name, he will be ushered into the land of the blessed, conducted by the Nyorai and Bosatsu. The picture is as splendid as it is rich in variety, minute attention having been paid to the details. The coloring also is gorgeous and attractive.

We can readily suppose that this picture, distinguished for its elaborateness of composition, served as a model for later painters of *raigō* art. This supposition is sustained by the "Shōju Raigō Zu" in Kōfukuji Temple and many other similar pictures, in which Amida Nyorai is accompanied by Kannon and Seiji and a group of Bosatsu on his trip to the earth. There are *raigō* pictures simpler in conception, in which the Nyorai have no other companions on his tour of salvation but Kannon and Seiji. These simpler pictures are perhaps in the majority. Some of these have great merit, such as the one entitled "Yamagoe Amida Zu," a picture of the Kamakura period, the valued possession of the Zenrin-in Temple. (Fig. 69) The picture is unsigned. It represents Amida, who, it seems, is compared to the rising sun, solemnly emerging from behind the mountains with a halo behind him. From his hands radiate lines, called *kechien*, threads of binding. Each person, in the world below, who holds the end of one of these threads is assured of salvation. The "Sō Raigō Zu,"

PLATE XIV   "Yamagoe Amida Zu"

(Collection of Mr. Y. Ueno, Ōsaka)

PLATE XV   "Sō Raigō Zu" (Chion-in Temple, Kyōto)

property of the Chion-in Temple, is notable because it pictures the idea of a speedy dispensation of salvation. The ordinary journey to the earth is too slow-moving to satisfy the wish of a devotee on his death-bed. So a fleeting cloud is used by the Nyorai as a carrier ; he comes down with lightning speed. Here the belief in salvation by religious people finds its strongest and most graphic expression. (pl. 15)

No discourse on Buddhist pictures would be complete without a reference to those relating to Nehan (Nirvana)—the death of Buddha. As many will agree, Buddha's death may be described as a happy and sublime end. It is free from the deep sorrow and misery of Christ's death on a cross, nor is it of the nature of Lao-tsze's end, which was marked by obscurity. Buddha died a glorious death surrounded by a group of many brilliant disciples, after a successful life of preaching the truth of spiritual emancipation and enlightenment to the people.

A " Nehan Zu " is always a picture which is bound to awaken in one the consciousness of a lofty life and a longing for the teachings of the great man. As a matter of fact, there are pictures that seem to meet such requirements satisfactorily. These arə the Nirvana paintings of the Kongōbuji Temple at Kōyasan and the Shin-Yakushiji Temple at Nara, both paintings belonging to the latter part of the Heian period. (Fig. 60) In the Kongōbuji picture, Buddha, clad in garments of bright gold and occupying the center of the canvas, is shown lying on his

bed, and breathing his last. Around the bed *shara*
flowers are blooming and a tiny stream is murmuring.
His disciples are these,—Shariho, Anan, Monju, Maka
Kashō, and others—and they are assembled to lament
the passing of their master. Some of them hang
their heads, some oppressed with deep sorrow, steal
glances at Buddha's face, others are sunk in silent

FIG. 60   "Butsu Nehan Zu" (Picture of Nirvana), Kongōbuji
Temple, Mt. Kōya, Wakayama

176 ～

grief! Such are the postures and expressions of the different characters in the pictures, but the pervading tone is the deep sadness of these persons who have thoroughly absorbed the philosophy of life taught by their master. This, however, is not the case in the Nirvana pictures of the succeeding Kamakura period. In them the sorrow of the disciples is exaggerated; some strike their heads, some roll about on the ground, and others shed tears of blood. This would seem the behavior of vulgar people, not becoming to disciples who have attained the spiritual status of a Bosatsu or a Rakan. So think the majority of the Japanese. This Kongōbuji picture, too, has evidently served as a model for later painters in compositions of Buddha surrounded by his disciples, for all following Nirvana pictures are invariably in the same mould. Almost identical in composition, for instance, is the "Butsu Nehan Zu" in the Shin-Yakushiji Temple. Only in this picture, the grouping of the disciples round the dying master is designed to produce a dramatic effect. The men are crowded in a small space, which has the effect of emphasizing the anxiety and restlessness with which the atmosphere of the death-bed is charged. It is interesting to note that in these two pictures only a single animal is introduced, while in other similar pictures, it is usual to see several animals here and there among the disciples. Tradition says that the twelve animals in the *jūni-shi* (Buddhistic Zodiac), that is, the rat, cow, tiger, hare, dragon, snake, horse, sheep, monkey, cock, dog, and hog, arrived on the scene in time to see the last moments of the dying Buddha. According to popular belief, it is because of this act that these animals have the honor of being used today in the indication of years, time, and direction.

The "Shaka Saisei Seppō Zu" (Shaka's Preaching on his Rebirth) of the Chōhōji Temple is a variation of the normal Nirvana picture, being based on a somewhat different tradition. The painter's name is unknown. When Shaka died and his mother, Maya-bunin, was informed of his death, she took the trouble to come down all the way from Paradise to earth. She stepped up to the gold coffin which contained his remains, and shed copious tears over it. Then, lo and behold! a miracle took place. The cover of the coffin opened by itself. Shaka returned to life and joined his hands in worship. At the same time, heaven and earth, which had been wrapped in darkness, were suddenly illuminated with a bright light. To console his mother in her sorrow, Shaka preached a sermon full of profundity and subtlety. The picture catches this inspiring scene. In the center Shaka, raising himself from his coffin, fixes his eyes on his mother, who, cane in hand, listens to the words of her son. Surrounding the pair, a number of Bosatsu, Rakan, and ministers stand with their eyes wide in wonder, dumbfounded by the glory of the dramatic situation.

Besides the philosophical and narrative pictures

FIG. 61 "Picture of Fudō Myōō" by Chishō Daishi

mentioned above, there are single paintings of Buddha or the Bosatsu that are intended, as in the case of similar sculptures, to be used as objects of worship. In every Buddhist family, a pictorial image of Amida, Kannon, Shaka, or Jizō is hung up in the altar. Among the masterpieces of this kind, the "Fudō Myōō Zu" by Chishō Daishi comes first to mind. (Fig. 61) Fudō Myōō (*Avalanathah*) is a Buddhist divinity, symbolizing the firm, unshakable mind that is resolved in the seeking after truth and salvation. He had a fierce heroic look as he stands on the rock of morality while flames of knowledge burst from his shoulders. In his hands he holds the sword of wisdom and a string to bind up temptations. Chishō Daishi (9th cent.) was a famous priest of the Shingon sect who lived in the early years of the Heian period. He is celebrated also as a painter and his artistic talent is plainly visible in the strength with which the bony structure and sinews of the figure Fudō is painted. In the picture he succeeds in giving a sense of the roundness of the human figure almost as clearly as in a sculpture.

Regarding the painting of this picture by Daishi there hangs a traditional tale. One day, so the story runs, as he was buried in deep meditation in the heart of Mt. Hiei, Fudō Myōō appeared to him and stirred him with inspiration. Strongly moved, he rubbed his forehead against the ground until it bled. Using the blood as paint he hurriedly sketched Fudō with the impression still fresh in his memory.

This is why the painting of Fudō's body is so red, and why people have taken to calling it "Red Fudō." There is another Fudō picture known as "Yellow Fudō." This was painted by a priest named Kūkō. Chishō Daishi is said to be the inspiration of this picture also. He again saw Fudō in a vision, and had Kūkō paint it according to his description. This Fudō is yellow in complexion and skin. The sinews are somewhat exaggerated, though not giving an impression of the grotesque. It has, however, a dignified presence and an air of spiritual energy.

In striking contrast with Fudō's pictures "Fugen Bosatsu Zu" in the possession of the National Museum in Tōkyō, a painting done toward the end of the Heian period, is characterized by feminine gentleness and elegance. It is exceedingly beautiful in coloring, and the body of the Bosatsu standing out in relief against the dark background is as exquisite as an ivory carving. The flowing red mantle hangs down from the green pedestal of a lotus flower and from its folds shapely legs peep out. The eyes which are as slender as threads and a mouth unusually small indicate, it may be presumed, the standards of beauty in those old days.

Fugen (*Samantabhadrah*) is a Bosatsu who was concerned with charity and prolongation of life, always riding a white elephant. He and Monju Bosatsu (*Manjusri*) form a pair of companions for Birushana (*Vairocana*). Birushana was Buddha in his manifestation as a brilliant sun. Translated freely the name is Dai Nichi Nyorai, or Great Sun Nyorai. His original is Shaka. The famous Buddhas at Nara and Kamakura represent Shaka in the phase. Monju is a Bosatsu credited with being conversant in all matters of knowledge. He is represented as riding a lion. A well-known painting of this sage Buddhist god is the " Monju Bosatsu " by Hirotaka Kose, a painter in the mid-Heian peiod. (Fig. 62) The lion in the picture is a product of the imagination, but it has strength and vitality suggestive of the king of beasts.

From what has been said so far it will be seen that Buddhist art in Japan, not taking into account the remote Nara period, produced the greatest number of masterpieces in the Heian period, with the Kamakura period coming next. There have not been any Buddhist pictures of great merit produced in the period subsequent to that time. Priests of the Zen sect, which was freshly introduced from China, painted monochrome pictures of Daruma, the founder of the sect, as has already been mentioned, but these are not called Buddhist paintings. In the Nichiren-shū and Shin-shū sects, which were founded in Japan and were the religions of the common people, it is to be presumed that there was no special incentive for the production of Buddhist pictures of high artistic distinction. There were picture scrolls illustrating temple histories or manifestations of Buddhist dispensation produced, but neither were considered as belonging properly to the class of Buddhist paint-

FIG. 62 "Picture of Monju Bosatsu" attribd. to Hirotaka Kose
(Daitokuji Temple, Kyōto)

～ 183

ings. The fact, therefore. is that not a single Buddhist picture of worthwhile merit has made its appearance in recent times. But it is perhaps too hasty to assert that the decline in Buddhist influence in Japan is responsible for this ebb in Buddhist painting.

X. SCENIC COLOR PRINTS

Travelers in foreign lands have reported that large cities in Europe and America now possess fairly large collections of Japanese pictures and that the majority of them are color prints. The Boston Museum of Fine Arts is noted for its excellent collection of the best examples of Japanese color prints. Fine collections of these pictures are also found in the possession of museums and individuals in London, Paris, the Hague, and other Western centers of population. Therefore visitors to Japan hailing from Europe and America may have opportunity to see specimens of Japanese color prints before they reach these shores.

Most of these prints were sent to the Netherlands in the closing years of the Edo period (1615—1867) from Nagasaki, which was the only port open to foreign trade in the days when Japan was closed to general outside intercourse. The only Western merchants who were allowed to trade with Japan were the Dutch, and it is easy to suppose that through them these color prints, after arriving in the Netherlands, would make their way further to London and Paris. Large numbers of these prints were sent out to China also from the port of Nagasaki. There are some indications that sometimes these prints were reproduced at Canton. From China these pictures may have been transmitted to Britain and France by the steamers of these nations. The export of color prints from Japan seems to have swollen in volume after the Restoration of Meiji (1868), when the number of Japanese ports open to foreign trade was increased, with a consequent increase in shipping traffic with Britain, France, Germany, America, and other countries. Japanese color prints caught the attention of many early Western visitors to Japan who were not only lovers of the exotic, but had a genuine appreciation of real artistic merit. They formed collections of Japanese color prints when the Japanese themselves were too distracted by the storm and stress of the revolutionary period to pay any attention to the preservation of the nation's art treasures. The result was that, when they realized the unique place the Japanese color print occupied in the world's art, they found that the collections of these prints abroad were far better both in quantity and quality than those in the country of their birth.

It is, however, a matter of some satisfaction to note that, through her color prints so widely introduced in the West, Japan has been enabled to make a contribution to the culture of the West, especially in the domain of the fine arts.

For example, one may mention " The Queen of the Pottery Land " by Whistler, who painted this famous picture from the inspiration he received from a beauty in a Japanese color print on view at the International Exhibition held in London about the middle of the 19th century. This picture shows a maiden standing before a folding screen clad in a *kimono* and with a fan in her hand. Perhaps this picture served as a model for the make-up of Madame Butterfly in Puccini's world-famed opera and also for the female characters in the *Mikado*. The consensus of Japanese opinion regarding the costume of the " Queen " is that it is a composite of the exoticism and the sartorial unfamiliarities that a foreigner sees in the beauties of Japanese color prints. A more important influence of the Japanese color prints on Western art is to be sought elsewhere. According to the views of prominent European art critics such as Goncourt and Mauclaire, for instance, painters of the French impressionist school, who ushered in the era of modern painting in Europe, derived some hints from Japanese color prints. It has to be understood definitely that this does not mean that the impressionist artists—Manet or Renoir, among others —who were fond of painting phases of the civic life of the Parisians immediately after the establishment of the Republic, which was characterized by festivity, enjoyment, peace, and tranquility, were influenced by the decadent delicacies with which the Japanese painters delineated their beauties. For in this the French artists had examples in abundance nearer at hand in the French rococo productions treating of subjects of pleasure and indolence. What the impressionists owed to the Japanese color prints was rather the manner in which light and atmosphere were captured in the scenic color prints by the landscape painters, especially by Hokusai and Hiroshige. As is well known it is the unique treatment of light and atmosphere that is the essential feature of the impressionists. The scenic color prints of Hokusai and Hiroshige slightly antedate the rise of the impressionist movement. The art dealer Durand-Ruel, who was a supporter of the impressionist school, held in his galleries at least two exhibitions of Hokusai's prints, presumably because he was aware of their importance in introducing the new trend in modern art.

A question may arise in the mind of the reader. How is it that Japanese painting, in which the technique of shading is unknown, could help Hokusai and Hiroshige produce the effects of light in their scenic color prints? How could such subtleties be achieved without the aid of the scientific European device of perspective? Well may such doubts arise. The truth is that not all scenic color prints show this modern technique. This effect was the result perhaps of special and accidental circumstances. Such is my interpretation. And to make my meaning clear, it is necessary to give a summary account of

" Fine Weather with Breezy South Wind "   by *Hokusai Katsushika*

the circumstances that attended the genesis and development of the color prints. Toward the end of the Edo period, the roads of the country, especially the Tōkaidō Highway were speedily improved, and this resulted in busy traffic over them, which in its turn led to the birth of the scenic color prints. It is not difficult to imagine that to the numerous *samurai* who accompanied their lords in their journeys to and from the feudal home towns, on and off duty in their services to the Shogun at the capital, and many merchants who traveled from Edo (now Tōkyō) and Ōsaka, and the pilgrims who made visits to worship at temples and shrines in various parts of the country, any scenic picture that would revive their memories of their travels should be cordially welcome. Color prints showing landscapes would also prove acceptable to visitors in Edo as souvenirs to friends and acquaintances. Those who received the gifts would in their turn be inspired with the desire to see with their own eyes the beautiful views the pictures presented, while those who felt the call of the wanderlust satisfied their longings with collecting scenic color prints which at that time had made their appearance on the market. These demands for prints were a great joy to the publishers of color prints, who encouraged and urged Hokusai and Hiroshige to produce more and more landscape prints showing new places of scenic attraction.

It must be noted that the painting of scenic views in various places of the country was not a new departure. The practice may be traced back at least to the Muromachi period (1392—1568). Such pictures were known by the name of " Meisho Zue " (illustrated guidebook of famous places). The subjects, however, were chiefly confined to scenic spots associated with shrines and temples that were popular with pilgrims because of the generosity of the deities enshrined therein in answering their prayers. The style of these pictures was mostly the *Yamato-e;* in them the device of the *kasumi* and numerous ornamental features were used. Not being realistic, the relative distances, for instance, between the front gate of the temple, the main hall, the belfry, the sutra depository, the priests' quarters, and the storehouse are not in the proper proportion. The structures themselves, too, are made to look far prettier than they really are. Such divergence from realism is a defect common to " Meisho Zue " done in Edo and in other places of note.

Somewhat different in nature are the landscapes of Hokusai and Hiroshige. First let us consider their subjects. Places of interest naturally take first place on the list. Hokusai's " Shokoku Meikyō Kikan " (Famous Bridges of Japan) (Fig. 63) and Hiroshige's " Edo Hyakkei " (One Hundred Views of Edo) and " Ōmi Hakkei " (Eight Famous Views of Ōmi) are good examples of this class. Both artists took great interest in Mt. Fuji and each made a series of thirty-six views of this internationally known peak viewed from different places. Though

FIG. 63 "Damask-girdle Bridge" from Hokusai's "Famous Bridges of Japan"

beautiful, however, Mt. Fuji was a sight almost too familiar as it could be seen almost every day from a dozen surrounding prefectures, and rather monotonous as it presented substantially the same view of the truncated cone from all angles. There is much more variety and interest in such pictures as Hiroshige's " Tōkaidō Gojūsan-tsugi " (Fifty-three Stages on the Tōkaidō) and his " Kiso Rokujū-ku-tsugi " (Sixty-nine Stages on the Kisokaidō). In these not only the well-known scenic spots, but little incidental scenes glimpsed on long travels are featured—a rustic station town, a long avenue of tall pine trees, a stone image of Jizō on the bank of a brook, and a hill unknown to fame and unexpectedly meeting the eye of the traveler resting on the veranda of a tea-house. Views such as these, needless to say, were far more appealing to travelers as souvenirs of their journeys in the past, for they possessed qualities which linked them with the everyday life and feelings of people. Themes of this nature aroused a warm feeling of affection in the hearts of the common people.

In their method of painting scenic color prints, Hokusai and Hiroshige depart from the rules followed by the illustrators of the *Yamato* school of art in painting the " Meisho Zue." There are exceptions certainly, and in the productions of Hokusai, for instance, he sometimes uses the *kasumi*, which is chiefly ornamental in purpose. But on the whole, the objective he aimed at was to be true to nature. Following the time-honored rules of Japanese paint-

FIG. 64 Mt. Fuji seen from Kanagawa   by Hokusai Katsushika

ing, the mountain and trees are outlined with brush-lines and there is also a complete absence of the shading used in European painting. Notwithstanding all this, a near approach to realism was the goal of the scenic color print artists. Distance is accurately proportioned, and no traces of sacrificing this accuracy for ornamental effects are to be found. In designing his compositions, Hokusai liked to take one by surprise, while Hiroshige preferred moderation. Though possessing such differences, these two masters of scenic art give no doubt of the fact that they both aimed at being realistic. For evidence one may point to the " Fugaku Sanjū-rokkei " (Thirty-six Views of Mt. Fuji) by Hokusai. These may be found in illustrated books of the " Meisho Zue " type, and as more excellent examples, in the productions of the monochrome masters of the Muromachi period, such as, Sesshū, whose famous Fuji picture is known as " Kiyomigata no Zu " (Picture of Kiyomi Bay). Motonobu Kanō and Tan-yū also produced paintings in which Mt. Fuji was featured. In all these works the majestic peak is painted with brush-lines preg-nant with force, but they show a deviation from the truth—the pair of curves on both sides which form the contour of the mountain are too steep both in their curvature and in their angle with the hori-zontal. The result is that, though the rare majesty of the noble peak is splendidly brought out, it is attained at the sacrifice of its natural form. They are Utopian idealizations of Mt. Fuji, fairy-like in

194 ～

association. In these masterpieces the traditions of monochrome landscape painting are faithfully followed.

Hokusai's Fuji pictures present a marked contrast to these. In his " Gaifū Kaisei " (Fine Weather with Breezing South Wind), showing the peerless mountain towering majestically, or in others, where the peak is glimpsed from among the angry waves (Fig. 64), or standing in relief against the sky above a white-walled storehouse in Nihombashi, Edo, or diminutively framed by a large wooden tub on which a cooper is working, the pictured cone always bears a fair resemblance to the mountain as it really looks. It is fairly evident that, in painting these pictures, Hokusai took the trouble to make actual visits to view Fuji on the Tōkaidō and the Kōshū-kaidō. The same must have been the case with Hiroshige. The two artists were no doubt equipped with a *yatate*, a Japanese penner, and sketch-books of their own make, with which they made rough sketches of Fuji on the spot. These sketches were transferred to large pieces of paper and the elaborate details filled in when the men were installed in their studios after returning home from a sketching tour. In Europe things were not much better for artists until the middle of the 19th century, when colors in tubes made in London began to be widely used. In the centuries antedating the mid-nineteenth century,—in the 17th and the 18th to be precise—Dutch landscape painters, even so handicapped by a lack of painting facilities, succeeded in producing works which perhaps no one can deny are realistic in the full sense of the term.

Realism can more readily be perceived in the scenic color prints of Hiroshige, whose style is more subdued than that of Hokusai. Both Hokusai and Hiroshige used the ordinary naturalistic presentation of landscapes which happened to take their fancy. Most artists would fear that this would result in common-place productions. And some of Hiroshige's landscapes certainly show such a weakness. To avoid the risk of becoming flat, they resort to various contrivances, one of which is variety in conception and design. As has already been mentioned, Hokusai combined Fuji with the roaring waves and with the framework of a tub in the making with the bottom still unlaid. Hiroshige in his landscapes conjures up poetic fancies in the atmosphere. Such devices are used most often. Both artists needed other devices to give freshness to their pictures, and this necessity caused the invention of their light effects. To them the light effects were no more than an interesting device in artistic expression ; they do not form as the keynote of all their productions.

This is naturally to be expected when one considers that, living in the latter days of the Edo period, they were utterly unacquainted with the theories of light and color formulated by Chevereul and von Helmholtz, on which the scientific stand of the impressionists was based. However, no one can gainsay that their pictures exhibit fine effects of light.

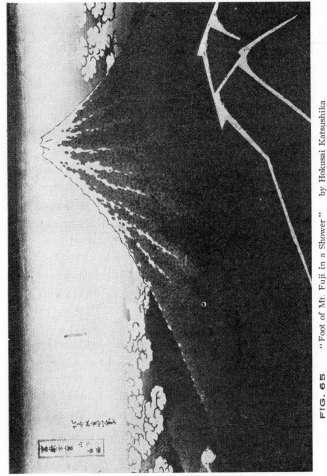

FIG. 65   "Foot of Mt. Fuji in a Shower"   by Hokusai Katsushika

In his Fuji viewed in the setting of dashing waves, one of the " Thirty-six Views of Mt. Fuji " to which reference has already been made, Hokusai succeeded in giving the impression of the strong light of mid-day at the height of summer. This he achieves by the strong contrast between the deep indigo blue of the waves and the bright yellow of the boat. In his " Sanka Hakuu " (Foot of Mt. Fuji in a Shower) (Fig. 65), another of the series, one senses the humidity of the surrounding and the light on the mountain differing in intensity from the dark grey of the base which is bathed in a summer shower and agreeable red brown of the summit. Perhaps more distinguished is another of his Fuji pictures—the " Gaifū Kaisei " already referred to. In this Fuji is painted delicately with trembling lines, towering against a clear sky. Its beautiful shape sets a new type of beauty for Fuji. It reflects the glorious light of the setting sun and shines in crimson radiance. Hence its popular title —" Aka Fuji," red Fuji. The picture catches the fleeting impression of twilight grey deepening and stealing over the extensive forest which covers the mountain at its base. Light effects as a device in art reached a high watermark in this picture, and it is no wonder that it served as a source of strong inspiration to painters of the impressionist school in France.

However, scenic color prints using light effects as a prominent feature are very few in number. Those showing interesting atmospheric effects are more numerous. These atmospheric effects are not of a scientific nature where, for instance, the subtle effect of reflected light is taken note of and an attempt is made to translate in the picture the atmosphere which veils the surface of an object. Rather it was chiefly the humidity of the air that the painter wanted to depict in his picture, probably because it served as a means of relieving the monotony of the scenic color print. We have seen how Hokusai in his Fuji picture entitled "Sanka Hakuu" tried to convey on paper the specific effect caused by the humidity of the air. In this print Fuji is exactly the same both in position and shape as it is in his "Gaifū Kaisei," but the two prints differ in effect. This must be because the difference in design makes them so radically different.

Prints by Hiroshige showing this atmospheric humidity are more numerous than those by Hokusai. In Hiroshige the atmospheric humidity is combined with a sort of poetic sentiment peculiar to the Japanese. To put it in another way, it is a source of the poetic sentiment to be seen in his productions. To confirm this statement with reference to Hiroshige's prints, I may mention the mist pictured in the stage-town of Mishima (Fig. 66) in the "Tōkaidō Gojū-san-tsugi" series, or that in the stage-towns of Nagakubo (Fig. 67) and Miyanokoshi in the "Kiso Kaidō Rokujū-ku-tsugi" series; the rain in "Tsuchiyama" (Fig. 68) of the "Gojū-san-tsugi" series, in "Ōhashi Bridge" in the "Edo Hyakkei" series, in

" Karasaki-no-matsu " (Fig. 69) of the " Ōmi Hakkei "
series; the snow in " Shiba Zōjō-ji " in the " Tōto
Meisho " (Noted Places of Edo) series. In Japan
bringing famous scenic spots into relationship with
the season, the time of day, and the atmosphere has
been an artistic practice since very early times.   A
typical instance is seen in the " Ōmi Hakkei " series,
the eight famous views of Ōmi province around Lake
Biwa.   These scenes are considered to be at their
finest when seen at the proper season and time.   Mt.
Hira looks prettiest when clad in snow and seen on
a winter evening; the Ishiyama Temple is at its
best when seen on a night touched by autumnal chill
and illuminated by a bright moon; the pine at Karasaki becomes heightened in beauty—so it seems to

200 ～

FIG. 67　　"Nagakubo"　　by Hiroshige Andō

the mind's eye—when the boom of a temple bell is
heard nearby in the utter darkness of night.　So say
the initiated.　This use of a natural phenomenon in
art is to be accounted for partly by the delicate
sensitivity of the Japanese to changes in the atmosphere and because of Japan's geographical position—
its situation in the temperate zone, known to the
geographers as the monsoon zone, and primarily,
because of the theories regarding scenic beauty laid
down by Chinese poets in connection with Lake
Tungting on the lower course of the Yantze-kiang,
and introduced into Japan.　It appears that the idea
appealed strongly to the Japanese poets, who at once
adopted them and set up similar scenic patterns in
the Ōmi Hakkei, substituting Lake Biwa for Lake

Tungting. The patterns served as a model for later poets in many of the rural districts, where, though remote from the centers of population, local versifiers poured forth poems in praise of the eight views of Ōmi.

This series on the beauties of Ōmi together with the seasons and the meteorological phenomena figure prominently in poems of the antique style and sometimes in paintings. These pictures, however, are not done in the realistic style. The snow on Mt. Hira gives no feeling of coldness; the autumnal moon at Ishiyama-dera does not suggest air agreeably free from moisture; the same lack of a realistic sensation might be said of the rainy night at Karasaki. However, in Hiroshige's "Eight Views of Ōmi" as

FIG. 68   "Tsuchiyama"   by Hiroshige Andō

rendered in color prints, there is, to a certain extent, a feeling of the atmospheric condition. In the "Pine-tree at Karasaki" particularly one senses the presence of a high temperature. Rain falling vertically, the grey of the ancient pine-tree standing beyond a sheet of dark indigo water but seeming nearer in the fore-ground—these make the onlooker feel the heavy pressure of air on his skin. He can almost hear the sound of the falling rain. This is an example of Hiroshige's masterly portrayal of atmospheric impres-sion and at the same time an expression of the poetic sentiment of the Japanese.

In this series of prints, Hiroshige expressed with good effect the spirit underlying "the eight views," which had been highly praised by poets but rarely

FIG. 69 "Pine-tree at Karasaki" by Hiroshige Andō

recognized by painters. In all his prints, the feeling of the seasons and the meteorological conditions are expressed in the form of the air temperature. The print depicting an evening shower at Ōhashi, already referred to, may be mentioned as the one which is the greatest success in this respect. It pictures a summer shower falling heavily on Ōhashi, a wooden bridge that crosses the lower course of the River Sumida in Edo obliquely. We gather that the shower is a sudden one from the long, straight, and slanting "feet of the rain" and from the confusion of the crowd hastily scudding in search of shelter. Beyond the river a wood is seen dimly, grey through veil of smoky rain, which suggests air heavily laden with moisture. Over it all hangs a dark, threatening cloud. The river, painted dark indigo, conveys the exact impression such an atmospheric condition would give. On the river there is a small long raft, forgotten there, and this adds a tinge of sadness to the scene.

Among Hiroshige's prints that emphasize the moisture of the air, and their number is by no means small, those representing snowy scenes seem to possess the greatest artistic merit. They also are most suggestive of modern art. The snowy view of the Zōjōji Temple at Shiba may serve as an instance. In this print there is a row of pine-trees, with their green fringes arranged rhythmically on the branches, standing on a long embankment in the foreground, and through the trees can be seen the two-storied

"Ōhashi in a Shower"   by *Hiroshige Andō*

vermilion gate, the main entrance to the temple. The roof of the gate, the branches of the pines, and the embankment are laden with snow. The artist shows the continued falling snow by white dots—made by the surface of the paper left unprinted—against the dark grey of the sky. The white of the snow, in contrast with the other colors used, the bright red and green, looks bright and ornamental. The snow itself is in bulky flakes, called " botan-yuki " (tree-peony snow) and makes a realistic picture. Looking at it one feels sure that the snow is moisture-laden as it usually is in the period of winter bordering on spring. What is it that gives such an impression? The answer is the small patches of light indigo blue added to white snow flakes in the print, which some how help to give that idea.

There are other examples of color prints in which indigo blue sets the snow to advantage. One of these is a triptych print entitled " Kisoji no Sansen " (Natural Scenery on the Kiso Highway), in which a blue stream runs at the foot of a snow-covered mountain with lifeless trees standing here and there on its slopes. The blue has the effect of intensifying the feeling of coldness produced by the snow. Anyone familiar with Hiroshige's prints will know that bright indigo blue is one of his favorite colors, so it is doubtful whether he was really conscious of the effectiveness of that color in setting off the pure white of the snow. It is, however, very likely that the French painters of the impressionist school picked

FIG. 70 "Lumber-market of Fukagawa" from the "100 Famous Places of Edo"   by Hiroshige Andō

up a hint or two about the effective use of color from his prints. This reminds one of the fact that Claude Monet, who was virtually the central figure of the impressionist group, learned the mystery of the use of color on inspecting a snow picture by Turner, the English painter, when he went over to London as a refugee in his escape from the Franco-Prussian War. The secret he learned was that snow looks more real and the cold seems to gain in intensity when it painted blue. Though Hiroshige himself might not have been conscious of the effect of color upon snow, Monet, as a keen colorist, could not have failed to absorb from his prints all that they had to give to the artistically trained eye.

In the foregoing I have described a few of the points in Japanese color prints which may have contributed to the art of the French impressionists. Besides color pints, Japanese paintings, sculpture, and works of the industrial arts viewed from new angles may contain features that can teach something of value to Western artists. If that be true, it is indeed a matter for deep satisfaction, for there is no greater pleasure than that of being of service to others in any capacity whatsoever.

LIST OF ILLUSTRATIONS

PLATES IN COLOR

CUTS

214 ～

INDEX

OF

CLASSICAL PAINTERS

Owing to limitation of space, only the painters referred to in this book, representative *ukiyo-e* painters and a few other noted artists are listed in this INDEX.

Re abbreviations:

S. School of painting to which the painter belongs.

L-C. Brief sketch of the life and career of the artist.

Sp. Speciality.

Aigai Takahisa 高久靄厓 (1796—-1843) **S.** *Nanga*
school. **L-C.** Born in Shimotsuke (now Tochigi
pref.). Studied painting under Tani-Bunchō,
the most famous *Nanga* painter at the time, in
Edo (now Tōkyō); greatly influenced by Ike-
no Taiga, one of the best *Nanga* painters, and I
Fu-chiu, Chinese artist. After traveling to
various places, he settled in Kyōto and finally
moved back to Edo. **Sp.** Landscapes.

Ando Kaigetsudō 懐月堂安度 (1671—1743) **S.** *Ukiyo-e*
school. **L-C.** Lived in Edo (now Tōkyō).
Founder of the Kaigetsu-dō school and one of
the outstanding figures of the early *Ukiyo-e*
school of painting (hand-painting, not printing).
Sp. Female figures.

Baiitsu Yamamoto 山本梅逸 (1783—1856) **S.** *Nanga*
school. **L-C.** Born in Nagoya. Went to Kyōto
where he lived for 23 years. Studied painting
under Kamiya-Ten-yū; influenced greatly by the
Chinese painters of the Ming and Ch'ing dynasties, especially by Chou Chih-mien. Nakabayashi-
Chikutō, famous *Nanga* painter and theorist,
was one of his intimate friends. Later, in his
closing years, came back to Nagoya where he
worked in the service of the lord of the clan of
Nagoya. **Sp.** Flowers-and-birds, landscapes.

Bunchō Tani 谷 文晁 (1764—1840) **S.** *Nanga* school.
L-C. Born and lived in Edo (now Tōkyō). Son
of a poet. Served Lord Tayasu as a painter.
Studied both *Nanga* and *Hokuga* paintings under

many masters and learned the Chinese (Sung, Yüan and Ming dynasties) and Western techniques of painting; created his own style of painting synthetically. Regarded as the best painter of that time. However, his works have decreased in value recently for some reason or other. **Sp.** Landscapes, flowers-and-birds, figures.

Bunchō Ippitsusai 一筆齋文調 (1725—1794) **S.** *Ukiyo-e* school. **L-C.** Lived in Edo (now Tōkyō). First studied the painting of Kanō school but later turned to *ukiyo-e*; much influenced by Suzuki-Harunobu. The peculiarity of Bunchō's color prints is due mostly to his realistic tendency. **Sp.** Kabuki actors, female figures.

Buson Yosa 與謝無村 (1716—1783) **S.** *Nanga* school. **L-C.** Born in Settsu (now Hyōgo pref.). When young, went to Edo (now Tōkyō), studied *haiku* or *haikai* (17-syllabled, short poem) and became a great poet. Loved painting, too. First, studied *Hokuga* painting, and later, influenced by Sakaki-Hyakusen and the Chinese *Nanga* masters, turned to *Nanga* painting. Regarded as one of the best and purest *Nanga* artists. Lived mostly in Kyōto and traveled to many places. **Sp.** Landscapes, *haiga* (sort of cartoon with *haiku* poem).

Chikuden Tanomura 田能村竹田 (1777—1835) **S.** *Nanga* school. **L-C.** Born at Takeda in Bungo (now Ōita pref.) and lived there. Son of a physician-in-ordinary. Served the Lord of Oka as a Confucian scholar. After resigning from his office, devoted himself to painting and calligraphy. In 1801, went to Edo (now Tōkyō) to study the technique of Tani-Bunchō, but, being dissatisfied with Bunchō's art, created a new style of his own. Visited Ōsaka and Kyōto many times and associated with noted painters, poets and historians. Became the greatest *Nanga* painter of the age. **Sp.** Landscapes, flowers, figures.

Chikutō Nakabayashi 中林竹洞 (1776—1853) **S.** *Nanga* school. **L-C.** Born in Nagoya and lived in Kyōto. Art-theorist as well as a painter. His son Chikukei 竹溪 (1816—1867) was also famous as a *Nanga* painter. **Sp.** Landscapes.

Chinzan Tsubaki 椿 椿山 (1801—1854) **S.** *Nanga* school. **L-C.** Born and lived in Edo (now Tōkyō). Watanabe-Kazan's ablest pupil. Being a *samurai* attached to the Tokugawa government, excelled in spearmanship and horsemanship; also played the reed-organ. Educated a son of his master, Kazan, after death of the latter. **Sp.** Landscapes, flowers-and-birds, figures.

Chōshun Miyagawa 宮川長春 (1682—1752) **S.** *Ukiyo-e* school. **L-C.** Born in Owari (now Aichi pref.) and died in Edo (now Tōkyō). First, studied the paintings of the Tosa and Kanō schools; later, influenced by the *ukiyo-e* of Kaigetsudō school, turned to *ukiyo-e* painting. Brilliant master of early *ukiyo-e* painting (hand-painting, not printing). **Sp.** Female figures.

Denzen Aōdō 亞歐堂田善 (1747—1822) **S.** Western-

style (*yōga*) school. **L-C.** Born and lived in
Fukushima pref. Studied *Nanga* painting under
Gessen, priest-painter, and at the age of 49 went
to Nagasaki and learned Western-style painting
and etching from a Dutchman. **Sp.** Landscapes
(etching and painting in the Western style).

Eishi Chōbunsai 鳥文齋榮之 (1756—1829) **S.** *Ukiyo-e*
school. **L-C.** Born and lived in Edo (now
Tōkyō). Eldest son of an upper-class *samurai*.
Served Tokugawa-Ieharu, Shōgun. Studied
painting under a Kanō-school master; later,
turned to *ukiyo-e*. After resigning from his post
in the government, became a prominent artist
in *ukiyo-e* printing and painting. One of the
representative artists of the golden age of *ukiyo-e*.
Sp. Female figures.

Eitoku Kanō 狩野永徳 (1543—1590) **S.** Kanō school.
L-C. Lived in Kyōto. Grandson of the great
master, Kanō-Motonobu. Served Oda-Nobunaga
and Toyotomi-Hideyoshi, feudal heroes. Painted
gorgeous and powerful pictures on the screens
and walls of Nobunaga's Azuchi castle and Hideyoshi's Juraku palace. The most distinguished
painter of the Momoyama period (1568—1615).
Very few of his works are left. **Sp.** Flowers-
and-birds, figures.

Ganku (Kishi Ku) 岸駒 (1749—1838) **S.** Kishi
school. **L-C.** Born in Etchū (now Toyama pref.).
After traveling to many places, settled in Kyōto
and attended the Imperial Court. Created his

own style but was too ambitious. **Sp.** Figures, animals.

Goshun Matsumura 松村呉春 (1752—1811) **S.** Shijō school. **L-C.** Born and lived in Kyōto. Studied poetry and painting under Yosa-Buson; after his master's death, associated with Maruyama-Ōkyo, master of realistic, black-ink painting. Founded a new school, taking the best points of Buson and Ōkyo. Also displayed fine skill in making *haiku* poems and in calligraphy. **Sp.** Landscapes, figures, flowers-and-birds.

Gyokudō Uragami 浦上玉堂 (1745—1820) **S.** *Nanga* school. **L-C.** Born in Bizen (now Okayama pref.). Served the lord of the clan of Nitta. After retiring from the service, started on an aimless journey with his sons, led a detached, Bohemian life playing the *koto* (sort of a harp); finally, settled in Kyōto, where he became intimate with Tanomura-Chikuden and other artists. One of the representative painters of the *Nanga* school; his paintings are marked with a vivid expressiveness and unworldly detachedness. Was also good at calligraphy and poetry. **Sp.** Landscapes.

Harunobu Suzuki 鈴木春信 (1725—1770) **S.** *Ukiyo-e* school. **L-C.** Born and lived in Edo (now Tōkyō). Studied *ukiyo-e* printing under Nishimura-Shigenaga; influenced by Ishikawa-Toyonobu. Originator of *nishiki-e*, and brought the Japanese color print to the stage of perfection.

His works are very elegant and refined. **Sp.**
Female figures.

Hiroshige Andō 安藤廣重 (1798—1858) **S.** *Ukiyo-e*
school. **L-C.** Born and lived in Edo (now
Tōkyō). The ablest pupil of Utagawa-Toyohiro.
After making genre prints, turned to a new
field, distinguishing himself as the great landscape painter of the Edo period—a poet of Nature
in color. Also skilled in hand-painting. **Sp.**
Landscapes.

Hirotaka Kose 巨勢弘高 (11th cent.) **S.** *Yamato-e*
school. **L-C.** Descendant of Kose-Kanaoka.
Famous as a Court painter, and one of the representative painters of the Heian period (794—
1186). Most of his works have been lost.

Hōitsu Sakai 酒井抱一 (1761—1828) **S.** Kōrin school.
L-C. Born in Edo (now Tōkyō) and lived mostly
there. Younger brother of Lord Sakai of Himeji.
At the death of his brother, refused the right
of succession and became a priest in Kyōto.
Studied the Kanō school of painting, *ukiyo-e* and
Nanga; later painted in the Kōrin style. His
works are noted for lightness and purity of color.
Also skilled in *haiku* poetry and calligraphy.
Sp. Flowers-and-birds, cartoons.

Hokusai Katsushika 葛飾北齋 (1760—1849) **S.** *Ukiyo-e*
school. **L-C.** Born and lived in Edo (now
Tōkyō). Pupil of Katsukawa-Shunshō; studied
many other schools of painting and created his
own style, both powerful and idealistic. Dis-

tinguished painter of the Edo period (1615—1867) and famous for his Fuji prints. Also skilled in hand-painting. **Sp.** Landscapes.

Hyakusen Sakaki 彭城百川 (1698—1753) **S.** *Nanga* school. **L-C.** Born in Owari (now Aichi pref.). One of the distinguished *Nanga* painters of the early period. Teacher of Yosa-Buson and skilled in *haiku* poetry. Lived in Kyōto. **Sp.** Landscapes, flowers-and-birds, figures.

Ichō Hanabusa 英 一蝶 (1652—1724) **S.** Hanabusa school. **L-C.** Born in Ōsaka and lived in Edo (now Tōkyō). Son of a physician. At the age of 15, went to Edo and studied painting under a Kanō master; later created his own original style. Being a man of fashion, frequently visited the gay quarters. Excelled in painting light and witty cartoons. Exiled to Miyakejima (Izu Islands) at the age of 47, lived there for 12 years. Painted many works while on the island and later in Edo. **Sp.** Genre painting.

Jakuchū Itō 伊藤若冲 (1716—1800) **S.** Created his own style by combining the good points of the Kanō and Kōrin schools and Chinese paintings of the Ming dynasty. **L-C.** Born and lived in Kyōto. Son of a greengrocer. **Sp.** Flower-and-birds.

Jasoku (Dasoku) Soga 曾我蛇足 (15th cent.) **Sp.** Muromachi *suiboku* school (black-ink painting). **L-C.** Born in Echizen (now Fukui pref.) and lived in Kyōto. Son of a *samurai*. Studied painting under Shūbun. Founder of the Soga school and an intimate friend of Priest Ikkyū. **Sp.** Landscapes, figures.

Kanaoka Kose 巨勢金岡 (9th cent.) **S.** *Yamato-e* school. **L-C.** Son of a high official. Founder of the Kose school and the most famous painter of that time. Painted, in 888, portraits of great Japanese Confucians on the screens of the Imperial palace. None of his works remain.

Kazan Watanabe 渡邊華山 (1793—1841) **S.** *Nanga* school. **L-C.** Born in Edo (now Tōkyō). A *samurai* of the clan of Tawara and served Lord Miyake. Pupil of Tani-Bunchō. Taking the good points of the *Nanga* and Western styles, developed his own style and became a distinguished painter of the Edo period (1615—1867). Well versed in poetry, Chinese classics and European sciences. As an official made great efforts to help the poor and to settle the financial difficulties of the clan. One of the most progressive and cultured statesmen of the Edo period. In 1839, falsely charged by the Tokugawa government, was confined to his home in Tawara and committed suicide in 1841. **Sp.** Flowers-and-birds, figures.

Kenzan Ogata 尾形乾山 (1663—1743) **S.** Kōrin school. **L-C.** Lived in Kyōto. Studied painting under Kōrin, his elder brother. Most skilled in making pottery (Kenzan ware) and versed in the tea ceremony. **Sp.** Flowers-and-birds.

Ki-en Yanagisawa 柳澤淇園 (1706—1758) **S.** *Nanga* school. **L-C.** Relative of Lord Yanagisawa of the clan of Kōriyama, Yamato (now Nara pref.) and the principal retainer of the clan. One of the founders of the *Nanga* school. Skilled in various arts and very sociable. **Sp.** Landscapes, figures, flowers-and-birds.

Kiyonaga Torii 鳥居清長 (1752—1815) **S.** *Ukiyo-e* school. **L-C.** Born in Uraga. Went to Edo (now Tōkyō) and ran a book-store. Studied *ukiyo-e* under Torii-Kiyomitsu and became his successor. The best of the Torii-school artists and one of the representative *ukiyo-e* artists. Also skilled in hand-painting. His works are rather realistic. **Sp.** Female figures.

Kōetsu Hon-ami 本阿彌光悅 (1545—1624) **S.** Created his own style. **L-C.** Lived in Kyōto. Born into the family of a sword-connoisseur. Studied painting under Kanō-Eitoku. The most distinguished, all-round artist of the Momoyama and the Edo periods. Skilled in calligraphy, pottery, gardening as well as in making lacquer-ware. **Sp.** Flowers-and-birds.

Kōkan Shiba 司馬江漢 (1747—1818) **S.** Western-style (*yōga*) school. **L-C.** Studied *ukiyo-e* under Suzuki-Harunobu ; learned the techniques of the Kanō-school and Western-style paintings. First painter in Japan to try copperplate engraving and one of the most important figures of the Western-style school. **Sp.** Landscapes, figures (*ukiyo-e* prints and Western-style paintings).

Kōrin Ogata 尾形光琳 (1663—1743) **S.** Kōrin school.
L-C. Studied the Kanō style painting, loved
the old Tosa-style painting and was deeply influenced by Hon-ami-Kōetsu and Tawaraya-Sō-
tatsu; originated his own style, free, elegant
and decorative. Excelled in calligraphy and the
technique of raised lacquer. **Sp.** Flowers-and-
birds.

Kunisada Utagawa 歌川國貞 (1786—1864) **S.** *Ukiyo-e*
school. **L-C.** Born at Katsushika near Edo (now
Tōkyō) and lived in Edo. At the age of 15,
became a pupil of Utagawa-Toyokuni the first,
and later studied under Hanabusa Ikkei because
of his love for Ikkei's great-grandfather Itchō.
Distinguished and versatile artist in the golden
age of *ukiyo-e*. **Sp.** Kabuki-actors, female
figures.

Masanobu Kanō 狩野正信 (1453—1490) **S.** Kanō
school. **L-C.** Born of a good family. Lived in
Kyōto. Studied painting under Shūbun and
greatly influenced by Liang Chieh of the Sung
dynasty. Founded the Kanō school. **Sp.**
Figures, landscapes.

Masanobu Okumura 奥村政信 (1690—1768) **S.** *Ukiyo-e*
school. **L-C.** Lived in Edo (now Tōkyō).
Pupil of Torii-Kiyonobu; influenced by Hishi-
kawa-Moronobu and interested in the scientific
method of Western-style painting. Excelled in
beni-e prints. **Sp.** Figures.

Matabē Iwasa 岩佐又兵衞 (1578—1650) **S.** Tosa school.
L-C. Son of a feudal lord who was killed in the
war. Lived in Kyōto when young, removed to
Fukui at the age of 45 and served Lord Matsu-
daira in Fukui. Invited to Edo (now Tōkyō),
painted for the Shōgun and died there. Skilled
in both the Tosa-style and Kanō-style paintings
and originated his own style. Also painted
fresh genre paintings and was believed to be a
pioneer of the *ukiyo-e*. **Sp.** Classical genre
painting.

Minchō (Chōdensu) 明兆—兆殿司 (1352—1431) **S.**
Buddhist painting and Muromachi *suiboku* school
(black-ink painting). **L-C.** Born in Awaji island
near Ōsaka. Became a priest when young.
Lived in the Tōfukuji Temple, Kyōto. Studied
the style and technique of the paintings of the
Sung and Yüan dynasties; one of the last masters
of Buddhist painting, and also was regarded as
a pioneer of the Muromachi *suiboku* school. **Sp.**
Figures, landscapes.

Mitsunobu Tosa 土佐光信 (1434—1525) **S.** Tosa school.
L-C. Lived in Kyōto. One of the three masters
of the Tosa school. Chief of the office of painters in the court. Painted many fine picture
scrolls.

Mitsuoki Tosa 土佐光起 (1617—1691) **S.** Tosa school.
L-C. Lived in Kyōto. One of the three masters
of the Tosa school. Chief of the office of painters in the court. Later, became a priest and

changed his name to Jōshō 常昭. Painted many screen pictures and picture scrolls. **Sp.** Genre painting, flowers-and-birds.

Morikage Kusumi 久隅守景 (c. 1700) **S.** Kanō school. **L-C.** Born in Kaga (now Ishikawa pref.) and lived in Kyōto. His life history is not well known. One of the four great pupils of Kanō-Tan-yū; did not confined himself to the Kanō school, freely and willingly accepted the influence of Sesshū. His works are elegant and serene and some of his landscape paintings even excel his master's works. **Sp.** Landscapes, figures, flowers-and-birds.

Moronobu Hishikawa 菱川師宜 (? —1694?) **S.** *Ukiyo-e* school. **L-C.** Born in Awa (now Chiba pref.). When young went to Edo (now Tōkyō) and died there. Son of an embroiderer. Studied painting of the Tosa school, loved and admired the paintings of Iwasa-Matabē; created an original style of genre painting and printing. Distinguished painter and the most important person in the establishment of a new, popular art, the *ukiyo-e*. **Sp.** Female figures.

Motonobu Kanō 狩野元信 (1477—1559) **S.** Kanō school. **L-C.** Born and lived in Kyōto. Son of Kanō-Masanobu. Served Shōgun Ashikaga. Married Tosa-Mitsunobu's daughter. Improved the technique of the Kanō school taking the best points of the Tosa school. **Sp.** Figures, land-scapes.

Musashi Miyamoto 宮本武藏 (1651—1712) **S.** Muromachi *suiboku* school (black-ink painting). **L-C.**
Born in Harima (now Hyōgo pref.) and died in
Kumamoto. Son of a *samurai* and the most
distinguished fencer in the history of Japanese
fencing. Also distinguished as a painter. His
teacher and career of painting are unknown.
His works are noted for their power, keenness
and simplicity.

Naonobu Kanō 狩野尙信 (1607—1650) **S.** Kanō school.
L-C. Born in Kyōto, lived and died in Edo (now
Tōkyō). Younger brother of Kanō-Tan-yū.
Influenced by the Chinese painting of the Sung
and Yüan dynasties, and more artistic than his
great brother Tan-yū, but unfortunately died in
mid-life (at the age of 43). Founder of Kanō's
at Kobikichō.

Nōami 能阿彌 (1397—1471) **S.** Muromachi *suiboku*
school. **L-C.** Formerly a *samurai* of Echizen
(now Fukui pref.). Lived in Kyōto and served
Shōgun Ashikaga as an artist. Studied painting
under Shūbun but the keynote of his paintings
is more mild than stern. Skilled in *renga* (verse
capping), the tea-ceremony and planning gardens;
also an excellent judge of paintings, tea-utensils
and calligraphy. **Sp.** Landscapes.

Nobuzane Fujiwara 藤原信實 (1176—1268?) **S.**
Yamato-e school. **L-C.** Lived in Kyōto. Son
of painter Takanobu. Poet and painter. Said
to have been an excellent portrait-painter of the

Kamakura period (1186—1392). Few of his authentic works remain. **Sp.** Portraits.

Nyosetsu (Josetsu) 如 拙 (15th cent.) **S.** Muromachi *suiboku* school (black-ink painting). **L-C.** Lived in the Shōkokuji Temple, Hyōto. Was treated with great favor by the Shōgun. Pioneer of the black-ink painting in the Muromachi period (1392—1568) and the predecessor of Shūbun and Sesshū. Only a few of his works remain.

Ōkyo Maruyama 圓山應舉 (1733—1795) **S.** Maruyama school. **L-C.** Born in Tamba (now Kyōto pref.) and lived in Kyōto. Son of a farmer. At the age of 15, went to Kyōto and studied painting under a Kanō-school teacher. Later, studying the realistic paintings of the Sung and Yüan dynasties, and applying the new methods of Western painting, achieved a realistic style and founded the Maruyama school. Very distinguished painter. Made many masterpieces and most of them remain today. **Sp.** Landscapes, flowers-and-birds.

Rosetsu Nagasawa 長澤蘆雪 (1755—1799) **S.** Maruyama school. **L-C.** Clansman of Yodo in Yamashiro (now Kyōto pref.). Lived in Kyōto. Studied painting under Maruyama-Ōkyo; the most distinguished follower of Ōkyo. Excelled in both rough and minute paintings. His imagination and composition in painting sometimes surpassed his master's. **Sp.** Landscapes, flowers-and-birds.

Sanraku Kanō 狩野山樂 (1559—1635) **S.** Kanō school.
L-C. Born in Ōmi (now Shiga pref.) and lived
in Kyōto. Studied painting under Kanō-Eitoku.
(His father was a pupil of Kanō-Motonobu.)
Adopted by Eitoku and became the successor of
the house of Kanō in Kyōto. Distinguished
painter ; painted gorgeous paintings on sliding
doors and screens but not very many of them
remain. Served Toyotomi-Hideyoshi, feudal
here. **Sp.** Flowers-and-birds, figures.

Sansetsu Kanō 狩野山雪 (1590—1651) **S.** Kanō school.
L-C. Born in Hizen (now Saga pref.) and lived
in Kyōto. Studied painting under Sanraku ;
adopted by the teacher and became the successor
of the house of Kanō in Kyōto. Distinguished
painter of the time. His works are rather
delicate and elegant. **Sp.** Flowers-and-birds,
landscapes.

Sesshū 雪 舟 (1420—1506) **S.** Muromachi *suiboku*
school (black-ink painting). **L-C.** Born in
Bitchū (now Okayama pref.). Became priest and
lived in the Shōkokuji Temple, Kyōto when
young. Pupil of Shūbun. The greatest master
of black-ink painting in the Muromachi period
(1392—1568). In 1467 went to China ; improved
his skill and enjoyed international fame. After
returning from China in 1469, made many
masterpieces, lived in Bungo (now Ōita pref.)
and Suō (now Yamaguchi pref.). The orthodox
school of black-ink painting in Japan was firmly

established by Sesshū. **Sp.** Landscape, figures.

Sesson 雪村 (1504—1589) **S.** Muromachi *suiboku* school (black-ink painting). **L-C.** Born and lived at Hetari in Hitachi (now Ibaragi pref.), later at Aizu and Tamura in Iwashiro (now Fukushima pref.). Became a priest when young. No details of his life are known. Most original and talented painter. **Sp.** Landscapes, figures.

Sharaku Tōshūsai 東洲齋寫樂 (18th—19th cent.) **S.** *Ukiyo-e* school. **L-C.** Lived in Edo (now Tōkyō). Actor of the Noh-drama in the employ of Lord Hachisuka of Awa. Painted chiefly portraits of Kabuki actors. Not recognized by the public in his lifetime. Today, however, he is regarded as one of the best *ukiyo-e* artists. **Sp.** Kabuki actors.

Shigemasa Kitao 北尾重政 (1738—1820) **S.** *Ukiyo-e* school. **L-C.** Born and lived in Edo (now Tōkyō). Studied *ukiyo-e* without a teacher. Worked for more than 50 years chiefly as an illustrator of story-books. Founded the Kitao school and did a great deal towards the revival of *ukiyo-e* in the beginning of the 19th century. **Sp.** Female figures.

Shigenaga Nishimura 西村重長 (1697—1756) **S.** *Ukiyo-e* school. **L-C.** Born and lived in Edo (now Tōkyō). Studied the style of Okumura-Masanobu and much influenced by Torii-Kiyonobu. Painted various subjects. Exerted a great influence upon Suzuki-Harunobu, Ishikawa-

Toyonobu and others. **Sp.** Female figures.

Shikō (Moto-oki) Watanabe 渡邊始興 (1683—1755)
S. Kōrin school. **L-C.** Lived in Kyōto. Served
Lord Konoe. Studied painting under the aus-
pices of the Kanō school, especially taught by
Kanō-Naonobu, and later found a great teacher
in Kōrin. Combining the best points of the
Kanō and Kōrin schools, became a unique painter
of the Kōrin school. Made fine black-ink paint-
ings with a slight pigmentation. Maruyama-
Ōkyo admired his works 30 years after his death.
Sp. Landscapes, flowers-and-birds.

Shōga Takuma 詫摩勝賀 (12th cent.) **S.** Buddhist
painting. **L-C.** Lived in Kyōto. Distinguished
painter of the Takuma school.

Shōhaku Soga 曾我蕭白 (d. 1781) **S.** Created his
own style. **L-C.** Born in Ise (now Mie pref.)
and lived in Kyōto. Studied the Kanō school
painting and the style of Sesshū. Admired Soga-
Jasoku. Originated a unique style of his own.
Very arrogant and particular; despised the art
of Maruyama-Ōkyo, great painter of the Edo
period. **Sp.** Figures.

Shōjō Shōkadō 松花堂昭乘 (1584—1639) **S.** Created
his own style. **L-C.** Born in Sakai near Ōsaka.
Became a priest and lived at the Otokoyama-
Hachiman Temple in Yamashiro (now Kyōto
pref.). Studied painting under Kanō-Sanraku
and greatly influenced by the Chinese paintings
of the Sung and Yüan dynasties; created his own

style. Skilled in both painting and calligraphy. Also famous as a man of refined taste. **Sp.** Flowers-and-birds.

Shōkei (Keishoki) 祥啓—啓書記 (15th—16th cent.) **S.** Muromachi *suiboku* school (black-ink painting). **L-C.** Son of a painter at Utsunomiya. Became a Zen-priest and lived at the Kenchōji Temple, Kamakura. Went to Kyōto for several years and studied painting under Geiami, son of Nōami. Distinguished painter of the Muromachi period. Loved pure black-ink painting. Many master-pieces remain. **Sp.** Landscapes, figures.

Shūbun 周 文 (15th cent.) **S.** Muromachi *suiboku* school (black-ink painting). **L-C.** Priest-painter. Lived in Kyōto. Studied painting under Nyosetsu (Josetsu). Distinguished painter of the Muromachi period (1392—1568). The great master Sesshū was his best pupil. His works are marked both by powerfulness and minuteness. Also very skilled in sculpture. **Sp.** Landscapes, flowers-and-birds, figures. (But all his works now extant are landscapes.)

Shūgetsu 秋 月 (d.c. 1510) **S.** Muromachi *suiboku* school (black-ink painting). **L-C.** Once a retainer of Lord Shimazu of Kagoshima. Later became a secular priest and studied painting under Sesshū, the greatest painter of *suiboku*-painting. Became one of the great painters of the time. It is believed that he went to China with his master, Sesshū. Lived in Yamaguchi

and in his last days went back to Kagoshima.
Sp. Landscapes, flowers-and-birds.

Shunshō Katsukawa 勝川春章 (1726—1792) **S.** *Ukiyo-e*
school. **L-C.** Lived in Edo (now Tōkyō). Pupil
of Miyagawa-Shunsui, son of Chōshun. Distinguished *ukiyo-e* painter and a leading character in
the revival formation of the *ukiyo-e* in the latter
half of the 18th century. His realism in *ukiyo-e*
exerted an important influence over both his
predecessors and his successors. Also skilled in
hand-painting. **Sp.** Kabuki actors, female
figures.

Sōami 相阿彌 (d. 1525) **S.** Muromachi *suiboku*
school (black-ink painting). **L-C.** Lived in
Kyōto. Pupil of his father, Geiami. Served
the Shōgun Ashikaga, succeeding his father and
grandfather. His work, like those of his father
and grandfather, is rather mild and refined
whereas most of the other *suiboku*-paintings are
marked with sternness and powerfulness. Also
famous as a tea-master and a gardener. **Sp.**
Landscapes.

Sosen Mori 森 狙仙 (1747—1821) **S.** Maruyama
school. **L-C.** Born in Nagasaki and lived in
Ōsaka. Studied painting under a Kanō-school
master but later changed his style to that of the
Maruyama school. His paintings of animals
(especially monkeys) were highly valued by
Maruyama-Ōkyo, great painter of the Edo period.
Sp. Animals, landscapes.

Sōtan Oguri 小栗宗丹(湛) (1398—1464) **S.** Muromachi *suiboku* school (black-ink painting). **L-C.** Feudal lord. After defeat in war, fled to Kyōto and became a priest of the Sōkokuji Temple. Said to have been a pupil of Shūbun or Kanō-Masanobu, great painters of that time. Very distinguished and seemingly one of the greatest painters in the Muromachi period. Very few of his works remain. **Sp.** Landscapes, flowers-and-birds.

Sōtatsu (Sōdatsu) Tawaraya 俵屋宗達 (17th cent.) **S.** Sōtatsu school or Kōrin school. **L-C.** Lived in Kyōto. Details of his life are not clear. Seemingly influenced by Kanō-Eitoku and the Tosa-school paintings. Sōtatsu and Kōrin were the most distinguished geniuses in the revival of the old *Yamato-e* painting. His works bear more open-minded dignity than Kōrin's. **Sp.** Flowers-and-birds, classical figures.

Taiga Ike(-no) 池 大雅 (1723—1776) **S.** *Nanga* school. **L-C.** Born and lived in Kyōto. Son of a fan-dealer. Loved painting and calligraphy since his youth. Influenced by Yanagisawa-Kien and the Chinese painter I Fu-chiu. Loved and studied the Chinese paintings of the Ming and Ch'ing dynasties. Became a distinguished painter and painted in the purely Japanese *Nanga* style. Also excelled in calligraphy and studied the doctrines of the Zen sect of Buddhism. Led a free and easy life, traveling to many famous mountains. Associated in a friendly and sincere way with many painters and writers. His works are marked by noble dignity and the most unrestricted freedom. **Sp.** Landscapes, figures.

Takanobu Fujiwara 藤原隆信 (1143—1203) **S.** *Yamato-e* school. **L-C.** Lived in Kyōto. Courtier. Distinguished portrait-painter. Also excelled in poetry. In his last years, became a priest. Among his descendants there are not a few *Yamato-e* painters excelling in portrait-painting. **Sp.** Portraits, figures.

Takayoshi Fujiwara 藤原隆能 (12th cent.) **S.** *Yamato-e* school. **L-C.** Lived in Kyōto. Courtier. Distinguished painter of his time ; became the chief painter in the court. Said to have painted pictures on the doors of temples and shrines, and also a portrait of ex-Emperor Toba. *Genji Monogatari Emaki* (a picture scroll) is attributed to him.

Tamechika Reizei 冷泉爲恭 (1823—1864) **S.** New *Yamato-e* school. **L-C.** Lived in Kyōto. Loyalist, serving the Imperial Court. Son of a Kanō painter. Loved old *Yamato-e* paintings and studied them without a teacher. Distinguished painter in the revival movement of the *Yamato-e*. Killed by a fervent loyalist. **Sp.** Classical figures, Buddhistic subjects.

Tan-yū Kanō 狩野探幽 (1602—1674) **S.** Kanō school. **L-C.** Born in Kyōto but moved to Edo (now Tōkyō) when young. Was a prodigy. Studied painting under his father Takanobu, son of the great Eitoku. Nominated painter-in-ordinary of the Tokugawa government at the age of 15. After the death of his father, studied under Kōi, the ablest pupil of his father. One of the most prominent painters of the Kanō school and the most famous and influencial artist of the Edo period (1615—1867). Today, however, his works are considered too formalistic. **Sp.** Landscapes, figures.

Tōgan Unkoku 雲谷等顔 (1547—1618) **S.** Unkoku school. **L-C.** Little is known regarding his life. Followed the style of Sesshū, the greatest *suiboku* (black-ink) painter of the Muromachi period (1392—1568). Founded the Unkoku school. Distinguished painter of the time. Served Lord Mōri as a painter.

Tōhaku Hasegawa 長谷川等白 (1539—1610) **S.** Hasegawa school. **L-C.** Born at Nanao in Noto (now Ishikawa pref.). Son of a dyer. Influenced by the paintings of the Soga school and later by Sesshū, the greatest *suiboku* (black-ink) painter of the Muromachi period (1392—1568). Distinguished black-ink painter. Also skilled in painting decorative polychrome pictures. **Sp.** Landscapes, animals.

Toyoharu Utagawa 歌川豊春 (1735—1814) **S.** *Ukiyo-e* school. **L-C.** Said to have been born in Bungo (now Ōita pref.). When young, said to have gone to Kyōto where he learned painting in the

Kanō-school style. Later went to Edo (now Tōkyō) and studied *ukiyo-e*; much influenced by Ishikawa-Toyonobu and created his own style. Founder of the Utagawa school. Skilled in both wood-block printing and hand-painting. Also created a new style of print, *uki-e* (picture in relief), in which he cleverly adopted the Western technique of perspective. In 1796, headed the group of painters commissioned to repair the Mausoleum in Nikkō. **Sp.** Female figures.

Toyohiro Utagawa 歌川豐廣 (1773—1828) **S.** *Ukiyo-e* school. **L-C.** Born and lived in Edo (now Tōkyō). Pupil of Toyoharu, also studied the Kanō-school style of painting. Competed unsuccessfully with Toyokuni. Teacher of Hiroshige. Illustrated many story-books. **Sp.** Female figures.

Toyokuni Utagawa 歌川豐國 (1769—1825) **S.** *Ukiyo-e* school. **L-C.** Born and lived in Edo (now Tōkyō). Studied *ukiyo-e* under Toyoharu from childhood. Influenced by Hanabusa-Itchō and Tōshūsai-Sharaku. Distinguished painter of the Utagawa school and most popular artist of the time. **Sp.** Kabuki actors, female figures.

Toyonobu Ishikawa 石川豐信 (1711—1785) **S.** *Ukiyo-e* school. **L-C.** Lived in Edo (now Tōkyō). Studied *ukiyo-e* under Nishimura-Shigenaga. Skilled in both wood-block printing and hand-painting. Often used another art-name, Meijōdō-Shūha 明篠堂秀葩. Very popular until surpassed by Suzuki-Harunobu. **Sp.** Female figures.

Utamaro Kitagawa 喜多川歌麿 (1754—1806). **S.** *Ukiyo-e* school. **L-C.** Lived in Edo (now Tōkyō). Pupil of Toriyama-Sekien who painted in the Kanō style and also excelled in *ukiyo-e* (hand-painting). Skilled in both printing and hand-painting. One of the greatest *ukiyo-e* artists. Mastered the technique of color prints with the utmost effect. In his last years, arrested by the Tokugawa government, imprisoned and died of illness. **Sp.** Female figures.

Yoshimitsu Tosa 土佐吉光 (13th—14th cent.) **S.** Tosa school. **L-C.** Details of his life are uncertain. Nominated as chief of the office of painters in the Imperial court.

Yūshō Kaihō 海北友松 (1533—1615) **S.** Kaihō school of black-ink painting. **L-C.** Born in Ōmi (now Shiga pref.). When young, became an acolyte at the Tōfukuji Temple and was greatly influenced by the teachings of the Zen sect of Buddhism. Lived in Kyōto. Studied painting under Eitoku and later turned to the paintings of the Sung and Yüan dynasties of China. Simplified the style of Liang Chieh, Chinese master, and, influenced by his training in Zen teachings, originated a new style of his own. Very distinguished painter in black-ink painting. Favored by Toyotomi-Hideyoshi, feudal hero, and painted on the screens of Hideyoshi's Juraku palace. **Sp.** Landscapes, figures, flowers.

GENERAL INDEX